My Big Box
Of Isobars

A Journey From Messy
Markers to Digital Doodles

André Bernier

Dedicated to:

My brother, Denié, who always encouraged me to pursue my dreams and who always took the time to look up at the sky with me.

And to all of my colleagues at WJW-TV and to all future media meteorologists.

Iron sharpeneth iron;
so a man sharpeneth
the countenance of his friend.

Proverbs 27:17
(KJV)

My Big Box Of Isobars

"What good is the warmth of summer,
without the cold of winter to give it sweetness."
John Steinbeck

"The wonder of a single snowflake outweighs the
wisdom of a million meteorologists."
Francis Bacon

"Another wonderful glimpse into the mind and life of one of the most accomplished meteorologists I was lucky to have had as a student, co-author and as a key part of the cable Weather Channel launch and success followed by a long and hugely successful career in broadcasting. Andre's multifaceted history included filmography and a faith-based Christmas novel series, "Christmas In Pilaf", and an autobiographical timeline, "The Extra Mile", a phrase which perfectly describes his career and life."
Dr. Joe D'Aleo, former professor of meteorology, Lyndon State College, Lyndonville, Vermont and co-founder of The Weather Channel.

"Andre Bernier's Big Box of Isobars hit home with me. Andre writes with the joy that can be found in people who see the majesty of the weather not as their God, but as a way to see God and get closer to God. The Book has morsels of delight, the musings of a man where weather is a stairway to Heaven.   A man who understands what a blessing the weather is. When you read this book, you will see Andre is part of a group that is the meteorological equivalent of Pastor Eric Liddle in Chariots of Fire. He famously said, "God made me fast and I feel his pleasure when I run." With Andre God made him for the weather, and he sees His majesty in the weather. And you will too! This book is a journey for those who have gratitude for the gift of weather. A wonderful read, and in a world gone mad, one that will make you happy you read it."
Joe Bastardi, Meteorologist, WeatherBell.com and frequent contributor to FOX News, WeatherJazz®, and many other media outlets.

My Big Box Of Isobars
From Messy Markers To Digital Doodles

André Bernier ©2024

Introduction

I used to hang on every word that WBZ-TV-4 meteorologist Don Kent uttered during his daily television weather broadcasts when I was in middle school and beyond. Don was in my 1970s superhero group along with a select few in both Boston and Providence television markets.

Fast forward thirty years. I was one of the early pioneers in podcasting when there was only one platform, Apple podcasts. After stepping on the toes of an already trademarked name for my very first episode, not only did I quickly change the name of the podcast for episode number two, but immediately designed a logo and successfully trademarked the name, WeatherJazz®.

One of my earliest interviews for WeatherJazz® was when Don Kent agreed to a telephone interview. It was such a delightfully long conversation, that I split it up and released it as a two-part series. During our hourlong conversation, one of the observations he made stuck out. Don said that he was especially grateful that he lived during a time during which he believed he saw the biggest and most significant advances in the field of meteorology that any of us had seen up to that point. As someone who was still involved in daily radio forecasting, he was right. But that was in 2008.

Fast forward again, this time to 2024. Now it's my turn to assess the progress of meteorology as I prepare to step off the prominent stage of television weather. I can now claim the same thing. Like with everything else that is technology-based, knowledge has increased exponentially since Don's graduation to heaven in 2010 at age 92. From the heavenly mezzanine (Hebrews 12:1), I'm sure he sees the exponential expansion as well as the growing pains that go along with it. That's how this book's subtitle came.

My very first reusable weather map was a birthday gift from my sister, Ninette. I was around eleven or twelve years old. She designed a double-sided map that was overlaid with transparent acetate. It came with water-soluble markers so that I could draw daily, and even hourly maps of New England and the USA. That map found a place in our finished basement near my study desk. That map saw years of daily and hourly action until I left that homemade weather bunker on September 3, 1977, to begin my college years in northeast Vermont.

By the time I started exercising my media skills on our college television station's daily newscast, both the New England map and USA map were full-body sized and painted in such a way that used water-soluble paint from a company called the Rich Art Color Company to draw our maps. A company that started in 1926, Rich Art is still in business today providing water-based paints and markers, nowadays mainly to elementary schools.

The markers to which I make reference were fat, stubby paint-filled plastic tubes with a

 fuzzy head where the paint was delivered to a surface. It was an ideal medium for drawing weather maps. It was high-contrast and color-rich, something the television cameras loved.

These markers followed me to my first commercial television position at WMT-TV-2 (now KGAN-2) in Cedar Rapids, Iowa in May of

1981. Even though WMT-TV was one of the very first television stations in the United States to use an 8-bit computer to generate a handful of our weather maps via "chroma-key," we also used the Rich Art markers to draw on a local Iowa map.

Even though the markers were water-soluble, washing the paint off the maps after every weathercast wasn't a task with which we were particularly thrilled. It required a bucket of water and several sponges or rags. I was lucky. Peter Smith, a perpetually joyful co-worker who was a part of the WMT-TV studio crew, always insisted to clean off my paint-rich maps after the noon newscast finished. When I was scheduled on weekends, the clean-up duties fell back on my shoulders. It was one of those messy duties that the television audience never saw.

By the time I moved to the launch team of The Weather Channel in March of 1982, founder John Coleman moved totally away from the messy boards. By necessity, we had to find a way to refresh graphics hourly since we would be on-the-air 24 hours a day.

The Weather Channel purchased the very first Quantel (electronic) Paintbox with a serial number of #1. By producing on-air weather maps using computers, refreshing the daily barrage of the maps needed for a round-the-clock network became far easier. The Weather

Channel set an new standard for television weather segments. Gone were the giant, messy markers, replaced by digital artwork drawn on digital graphics tablets. It was a quantum leap in the way we visually told the weather story on television.

When my final career move took us from Minneapolis to Cleveland, I had the privilege of working with Dick Goddard. He was 57 years young when I arrived in January 1988. While he contemplated and spoke about retirement as he approached 65, his tenure would last over 50 years, far longer than anyone expected.

Dick had a bit of a love-hate relationship with computers. While he enjoyed the wider degree of creativity it offered his artistic skill, we all heard him mumble under his breath every time we had a software upgrade or a new computer system.

"Oh boy," he would say, "just what we need. Another computer downgrade."

Since graphics computers had entered into the scene of television weather just as I took my first job in Iowa, it was an exciting time for broadcast meteorologists. I took to the new technology like a duck to water, even helping weather graphics companies develop and improve weather systems like the Kavouras i7 and Silicone Graphics' "O2" and "Octane" based systems.

As I approach my 65th trip around planet Earth, computer systems are becoming exponentially more complex, so much so that (quite suddenly!) I'm starting to understand why Mr. Goddard hated software and computer "upgrades!" Trying to keep up with my younger, computer-savvy colleagues takes concentrated effort. What used to be second-nature now takes intentional discipline. There are days when I wish I could draw a camera-ready weather map with a set of Rich Art Color markers!

I've had a blessed, God-directed career starting with seven years in radio (beginning at age 15 at 1420, WBSM-AM in New Bedford, Massachusetts). I'll cap off my career with more radio work with WKJA-FM (91.9 MhZ), Cleveland (also known as "Heartfelt Radio"). The benefit nowadays will be to work from my home studio without the need to put on a suit and tie and to greet and inform people in their kitchens and cars with a coffee cup in my hand, even wearing pajamas and sporting creative "bed hair!" (My apologies for destroying that pristine image of what morning radio may "look" like.)

It's a great way to slide into home plate after stealing second base (more than once!) and being the RBI for a truly great weather team now getting ready to score big for the FOX 8 team.

What you are about to read is not your typical memoir. It is not a chronologically arranged, events-based read. After signing my most recent (and final) contract with FOX in January 2023, I started journaling those things related to my near half-century professional career that came to mind. Some are stories I'll never forget. Others were delightful surprises, memory fragments from well before I took to the radio airwaves on 1420-WBSM. As the Lord brings them to my recall, and as I draw closer and closer to closing the television chapter, I hope you will be able to step back and see the completed piece of artwork when I put the paintbrush down.

In the meantime, enjoy the process with me. A little bit here. A little bit there. A dab of blue sky and clouds. A shard of green grass and dollop of wildflowers. The daub of a distant landscape. One concentrated and deliberate stroke at a time until the painting is finished.

Even though famous PBS artist Bob Ross created more than 30,000 individual paintings, I'm certain that he would support and approve of my resolute calling, that is, to concentrate on this single work of art. After all, isn't every single life lived for the Lord a work of art?

Friday, January 13, 2023
9:04 AM, Light Snow, 29°F (2" New Snow)
Mile Marker 495

Dateline: Thursday, January 12, 2023, 3:30 PM —
Delightful meeting with Andy Fishman results in
agreement to extend current contract to the final
day of the May 2024 ratings book, the date upon
which I will hang up my television isobars.

As of today, 495 days until a new chapter begins
(May 22, 2024). I'm at perfect peace with this and
sense God's pleasure.

I'm now looking back at a career that went through
so many God-directed detours to help me grow, at
times a process that was more than uncomfortable.
If it wasn't for God's grace and the knowledge of His
presence during those episodes, I would have
jettisoned this God-chosen path for my life long ago.
Had I given up, I would have missed so many
blessings along the way, especially those enjoyed in
recent years....

....thinking back to the day Mom and Dad released
me to the world after graduation from Lyndon State
College just before Sally drove me from New Bedford
to Cedar Rapids (where I waited to buy my first car,
a 1981 2-door Mustang), I can still hear Mom's
words of release: "Now go... and make something
out of your life!" She meant these words to be
encouraging, supportive, loving, wanting to say
something that I would always remember. Indeed I
have, even more so as the chapter that she initiated

with these words of blessing will come to a close in 495 days.

"Make me proud," she also said.

I'm confident that you are, Mom... as you watch this home stretch from heaven's mezzanine! Thank you for all that you and Dad did to give me such a great foundation for my journey.

Tuesday, January 17, 2023
9:19 AM, Cloudy, Murky, 42°F (CC Remains)
Mile Marker: 491

Book idea... developing. Stay tuned.

Wednesday, January 18, 2023
9:04 AM, Foggy, Murky, 35°F (Bare Ground)
Mile Marker 490

After numerous failed attempts, I'm trying again. Is my first TV weather news director-boss Bob Jackson still around? I sure hope so. I'd like to honor and thank him for taking a chance on me by hiring me for a weekend weather slot at WMT-TV-2, Cedar Rapids, Iowa 42 years ago, even before I graduated from Lyndon State College. He offered me the job after flying out to Iowa from Burlington, Vermont airport. I was in Iowa Sunday, March 29, 1981 to Monday, March 30, 1981. The interview was over and I was offered the job just as commotion broke out in the newsroom: then President Ronald Reagan had been shot in an assassination attempt at the Washington Hilton after a speaking engagement. (I can replay the scene in my mind's eye with clarity, even more than four decades later.) By the time I retire next May, it will have been 43 years ago that my television weather career began... almost to the date!

Monday, January 23, 2023
9:55 PM, Cloudy, 27°F (4-5" Remains On Ground)
Mile Marker 485

Signed contract delivered to (news director) Andy today. I also spent 30 minutes talking to Paul Perozini (GM) to thank him for extending such wonderful courtesies to me. I wish I would have learned how to be myself and relax when having audience with news directors and general managers when I was younger. My guess is that it's something that matures over time. It just seemed to develop much more slowly for me.

Thursday, January 26, 2023
7:56 AM, Blowing Snow, 30°F (CC New; 2" OG)
Mile Marker 482

Just before my workday ended yesterday, I did some internet digging hoping to get a contact to invite pop singer Michael Johnson as a WeatherJazz® guest. I was shocked to learn that he died in July 2017 from heart and lung disease in his home state of Minnesota. I was also surprised that he was 72 (would have been 78 today)... I thought he would have been a little younger. More surprises include the number of albums he released in his career! I'm familiar only with his self-titled album from 1977-1978 on the EMI label. I listened to some of his other releases on my way home from work last night. So much talent! I wonder if he is using his talent to praise God in heaven? I sure hope he said 'yes' to Jesus. I'll remain hopeful that he can be a guest on a heavenly version of WeatherJazz® someday.

His folksy, down-to-earth songs on his 1978 album were so easy to relate to. Simple life pathways. Simple decision points. Relatable life missteps and their consequences. Simple desires for a magical life partner. It was (and IS) such an easy collection in which to get absorbed.

Friday, January 27, 2023
8:34 AM, Stray Flurries, 23°F (1" New; 4" OG)
Mile Marker 481

I'm relishing the thought of looking at where the Lord led me in my career timeline in context of the puzzle pieces that came together to make this amazing life snapshot! I've already thought of events and moments that have escaped my attention for decades, yet each played an important role in shaping my journey.

Monday, January 30, 2023
8:22 AM, Flurries, 26°F (CC New; CC-1" OG)
Mile Marker 478

A recent Facebook post surprised me last week. News about Cedar Rapids' WMT-2/KGAN-2 longtime news anchor, Dave Shay, surfaced. Still alive? Yes! And thriving having just celebrated his 94th birthday in Minneapolis. Wow. I was so fortunate to work with Dave for a short season at my first television job out of college. Dave truly embodied the word, "professional," in every way. He was a stickler for spelling. I can see him in my mind's eye, sitting with the Chyron operator (electronic font machine), going through every frame to check for spelling errors before the newscast. That's something I haven't seen since. Perhaps that would have prevented an error I saw during Sunday's NFL football game that promoted this year's Super Bowl occurring on February 29! There IS no February 29 this year. It should have read February 12.

Tuesday, January 31, 2023
10:32 AM, Mostly Sunny, Cold, 16°F (1" OG)
Mile Marker 477

During the night, I had a dream about writing Virgil Dominic a letter, letting him know that I was retiring. Virgil was 53 years young when he hired me in January of 1988. He is 88 today and enjoys life in NEOhio. I am so grateful that he took a chance on me 35 years ago. I am most grateful that he is a man of God. His faith walk is evident. I see the dream as a nudge from God to encourage him with my grateful view of my career, now 35 plus years in the rear view mirror.

Sunday, February 5, 2023
7:51 AM, High Overcast, 39°F (Cosmetic Marbling)
Mile Marker 472

Seems like I have hit yet another dead end in my search for my first television news director, Bob Jackson, from then WMT-TV-2, Cedar Rapids, Iowa. Even though I had a wonderful and redeeming conversation with Bob in his Magid Consulting office sometime in the 1980s, it seems like I'll be missing a very important piece of the story by not including Bob in this reflective period between now and May 22, 2024. I wonder how he has been able to slip through our tight-knit network of television news people on social media?

Thursday, February 9, 2023
8:47 AM, Rainy, 45°F (Trace Snow On Deck)
Mile Marker 468

Yesterday morning, I woke from a strange dream where I was finishing up my final TV weather segment before retiring. Upon walking into the newsroom, Andy came in with a few gifts to give me in front of everyone in the newsroom. I saw that one of the items was a large commercial bag of flour.

How strange! What was THIS all about? I never got the chance to find out since I woke before Andy presented me with the flour.

Friday, March 10, 2023
10:14 AM, Light Snow, 33°F (Just Under 1" New)
Mile Marker 439

When computers and their programs run well, it's a fun thing. When trouble arises, it's a time sucker....

The snow arrived on time (4 AM) today, but very little accumulated until after sunrise. So far, it's a lovely snow. No need to use the snow blower or shovel.

After crafting my own 1981 playlist on Spotify, I found myself remembering things from my first job in Cedar Rapids, Iowa, while listening to the songs on my way to and from work. Aside from being so far away from New England, WMT-TV-2 was an amazing place to work. I had to pinch myself many times to remind myself that my career would begin in an eastern Iowa town that seemed to fit my personality in so many ways, let alone in market size #74 (in 1981 as best as I'm able to remember). Nowadays, the Cedar Rapids-Waterloo market size is #92. (Did they lose that many people in four decades?)

After graduating in early May of 1981, Sally joined me in heading to New Bedford to gather some essentials before Sally drove me out to Iowa. I looked for a car to purchase in New Bedford, but didn't find exactly what I was looking for. Not only that, I ran out of time needed to register in a state that I would only have to change immediately when I drove to Iowa. It was a headache I did not need.

Mom really wanted me to stay long enough to celebrate my 22nd birthday on May 22, but I was feeling the pressure from WMT-TV to come to Iowa as quickly as I could after graduation. I didn't want the management team to have the added irritation of waiting another week for me to begin my employment. They were anxious for me to come and bring relief to Dave Towne, Barry Norris, and Lee Dennis. As sad as Mom was to not celebrate my birthday in person, she understood what I needed to do. I sensed both sadness and great pride that I landed a highly coveted dream job.

"Make me proud," she said moments before Sally drove me down Sutton Street to Shawmut Avenue on my way to I-90 West. I prayed that I would be able to do that... and it gives me satisfaction to know that I was able to deliver that, and hopefully more.

Saturday, March 11, 2023
6:50 AM, A Lazy Flurry, 27°F (Cosmetic Coating)
Mile Marker 438

Yesterday, Dontaé and I were talking about the simplicity of raw appreciation for weather, not the kind that hovers over model data, radar loops, and the like. It's the kind of fascination of weather that sends you flying out the door to watch a thunderstorm roll into your neighborhood from your driveway. As a television meteorologist, those days are limited mainly to when you have a day off and something interesting is happening in the sky. As I approach them moment when I hang my television isobars on the FOX 8 coat rack and leave them there, returning to the days of enjoying the raw love for weather of all types is beyond appealing.

Some of my fondest and earliest memories of being captured by the enthrallment of what the atmosphere was tossing my way includes coming home from New Bedford High School as a freshman as a 13-year-old. It was a cold and windy March day. The irritated cumulus clouds drove me to hoping at least one of them would release a snow shower or two. Homework would have to wait.

After putting my books and assignments inside from walking the 1.1 miles from the high school to our house, I raced back outside. There was a certain tree in the wooded area behind our house that was a favorite perch from which to watch life go by. It was big enough to support my weight, but small enough to have nearly horizontal branches that were easy to climb. I hung a traditional liquid-in-glass thermometer at eye-level from my perch some six or seven feet from the ground. The view of the sky from there was grand.

After a few minutes or so, I noticed that one of the built-up cumulus clouds was getting quite dark at the base. Could this escort snowflakes in? A check of the thermometer confirmed that it was certainly cold enough at 34°F.

As the sun disappeared behind the cluster of wintry-looking clouds, the wind picked up. I pulled out my hand-held wind measuring device. Gusts approaching 20 m.p.h. Eventually, the darker sky offered what I was hoping to see. Looking northwest, the first few snowflakes started falling near the house. I watched as the curtain of snow moved into the woods. I smiled as the snow swirled about me and the wind rocked the small tree back and forth enough that I could feel it. I checked the thermometer again. 33°F.

The snow shower lasted no more than a few minutes. It was long enough to put down a very light signature of snow on the backyard lawn and woods floor. After the wind let up and the sun popped back out, the wintry artifact disappeared. Would another snow shower come through? I waited patiently from my perch for what seemed like a small eternity, wondering if Mom saw me in the tree. She probably did and knew that I would be there to greet any snow shower that swooped by for a visit.

As best as I can remember, the process repeated once or twice more. Now THIS was exciting! Better than any movie or television program. It was an atmospheric drama unfolding in front of me. Eventually, my brother Denié arrived home from Normandin Junior High on the bus, joining me in "the woods" to blow off some steam before we got cold and retreated inside for an after-school snack and to start tackling homework.

While my tree-climbing days are we'll behind me, getting back to enjoying the raw elements of weather, that which called me into a career of tracking all kinds of atmospheric mischief, is something to which I'm soon looking forward.

Sunday, March 26, 2023
7:56 AM, NACITS, 33.3°F
Mile Marker 423

March 25th is always a special date. For as long as I live, I'll forever pause whenever I wake up on March 25th. It's one of those "life's turning points," not because today would have been Mom's 101st birthday (although that is frosting on the cake).

Being a lifelong meteorologist, I remember certain days in context of what the weather was like. Friday, March 25, 1977 (Mom's 55th birthday) was a wild weather day. There was a big storm just off the coast of Boston. It was very windy and becoming quite cold. I pulled up an archive weather map from NOAA from that day and confirmed that.

I had a planned day off from high school. I was a senior. Mom took the day off from work so we could visit Lowell Tech in Lowell, MA as a possible college choice. We were up early (5 a.m.) for a planned visit to see meteorologist Bob Copeland at WCVB-5 on our way to Lowell.

Side Note: Bob retired from TV long ago and is now 90 years-old and lives in northern New Hampshire. Bob operated an artist studio for many years following his retirement. He is a gifted painter. I commissioned Bob to do a painting for me of my view of Burke Mountain from my Lyndon State College dorm room, a painting I gifted to Denié.

The tour that Mom and I had was eye-opening for both of us. The meteorology department was ill-equipped. As much as Mom had hoped I would be closer to New Bedford for my college years, she quietly leaned over at one point and said, "Wow. Your weather equipment at home is far better than what they have here."

One of the highlights and lasting memories of that day was retreating to the car to have lunch. We enjoyed the sandwiches that Mom packed with the hot coffee from a big thermos as the strong, cold winds rocked the car back and forth. We had the car AM radio on in the background, set to 680-WRKO (Boston). One of the songs that played was Al Stewart's first big Top 40 hit, The Year Of The Cat. (Whenever I hear that song now, I'm immediately transported to that moment in time.)

During our mid-afternoon drive back to New Bedford (about 90 minutes), we stopped at Howard Johnson's for hot soup. The cold wind had chilled her to the bone and hot soup sounded great to both of us. By the time we arrived back at 78 Sutton Street, it was clear that Mom's chill was the start of a flu virus that sent her immediately to bed while she insisted I head to the Wonder Bowl to meet up with my bowling teammates for our Friday afternoon league. Just before that, my sister Henriette and her young daughter Beth arrived with a birthday cake that was decorated by Beth. The frosting was a dull gray. On any other day, Mom would have fussed over the rather unattractive cake recognizing the love with which it was made, but on this day, one look immediately sent Mom to the bathroom. I had to explain to the both of them that Mom was sick. She meant no offense to the (really ugly) cake.

Fast forward to 3:30 p.m.

I arrived at the Wonder Bowl just as our league started the 5-minute practice period called "shadow bowling." I made it. My then girlfriend at the time was on the league, too (to this day I'm thankful that we remain very good friends). She was anxious to hear about my college visit. I had to tell her that Lowell Tech was out of the running. My main focus was now in northeast Vermont, some three times farther away. I could see the disappointment. It was a life turning point that cascaded to many hairpin switchbacks in the next few years.

Over the decades, it has been tempting to wonder what life would have looked like today having made different choices, but the longer I journey on this earth, the more slippery that slope becomes. In hindsight, would I have loved being a better... son, brother, employee, classmate, boyfriend?

Absolutely!

Yet, regrets are an interesting thing. I'll forever remember a Danny Devito quote as the character Phil Cooper from the film, "The Big Kahuna" (1999), where he said: "...you've already done plenty of things to regret. You just don't know what they are. It's when you discover them, when you see the folly in something you've done and you wish that you had it to do over, but you know you can't because it's too late."

Sigh So true.

But I've also made peace with (even some of the careless) choices I made in my approaching 64 years.

Would I have had a near fifty-year career in broadcast meteorology, some of it on national television? Would I have heard God's call to minister to people? Would I have a blessing of a son, Noah, and an amazing wife who has given me so much grace over the decades? Would I ever have bonded so tightly with special lifer friends including a host of special people in Iceland just to name a few?

Unlikely, and I can't imagine life without each of them.

See what I mean about the slippery slope of "what if?"

Friday, March 31, 2023
9:24 AM, Showery, 40°F
Mile Marker 418

I find it ironic that forty-two years ago this day in 1981, I was back on campus at Lyndon State College (Vermont) having just returned from my flight to Cedar Rapids for an in-person interview at WMT-TV-2, the CBS affiliate, for a weekend weather job there. After so many standard rejection letters from stations in New England (including one from a tiny television market in Johnstown, PA), I was truly excited to have any station interested in hiring me, even if it was a thousand miles away from home.

The reason became apparent when WMT-2 news director Bob Jackson popped my three-quarter inch video tape resume in his machine to watch it. It wasn't my best work, but I was highlighting many agricultural impacts of the weather pattern, a topic that drew their attention. I would have never sent them that reel had I realized what weathercast I was sending him... but it was THAT reel that made me stand out! God was clearly moving on my behalf. Cedar Rapids was where God wanted me. At that point, I had no idea why. In the end, the reasons were many but would not be clear to me during may tenure in eastern Iowa.

On Monday, March 30, 1981, my interview was suddenly over when pandemonium broke out in the newsroom. President Ronald Reagan had been shot after speaking at a luncheon. I was offered the job and given a contract. Suddenly, it was as if I was invisible as everyone in the newsroom was scrambling about. I can't remember who drove me back to the airport to catch my afternoon flight back to Burlington, Vermont with a connection in Chicago. Sally had a car on campus and drove to Burlington to pick me up. I think another classmate was with her to keep her company on the ninety-minute drive since my flight would arrive back in Vermont well after dark. I returned to my college campus, more than a month before graduation, with a job waiting for me in Iowa. Despite being so far away from "home," I was on cloud nine. Staying focused on the homestretch of my academic assignments was a little bit of a challenge, but something I obviously navigated.

Sunday, April 23, 2023
8:07 AM, Beautiful Sunrise, Crisp, 36°F
Mile Marker 395

I woke Saturday to the peaceful sound of heavy rain rhythmically pounding out delightful white noise on our metal roof and skylights. It was unusually dark as well. As I sipped on my first cup of coffee and engaged Bill Martin in our online Bible study, one of those great random memory fragments came flooding into my mind, one that I have shared with others on many other occasions.

The sound of the cool rain propelled me more than five decades into the past. With clarity, I am in the backyard vestibule at 78 Sutton Street in New

Bedford, my boyhood home, watching and hearing the heavy rain come down. It's was a Sunday morning. The television was on with the opening theme from ABC-TV's science program, Discovery, filling the house. (This had to be when I was in elementary school since Discovery was canceled in September 1971. I can still hear the theme song in my head as clear as day.) Watching the heavy rain was fascinating. I can remember watching my home built anemometer that was installed very high up on a very tall pole on which the end of our clothes line was suspended near the garage. The aroma of Mom's Sunday dinner was starting to fill the house. I had a front row seat as I watched the wild rainstorm from our cozy cocoon.

I still get that sensation watching all kinds of weather events from the cozy confines of our home. The meteorological show is always free and the surroundings (hopefully) cozy, peaceful, and safe.

Saturday, April 29, 2023
6:46 AM, Cloudy, Foggy, 49°F
Mile Marker 389

Foggy mornings like this will always take me back to the fog that fascinated me as a youngster in southern New England.. Like this morning, those days were always quiet and cozy in a way that invited me to enjoy God's atmospheric "hug." Only days after getting settled in my dorm room as an incoming freshman in northeast Vermont, I was up hours before sunrise to file a week of morning radio forecasts by phone for my hometown radio station, 1420AM-WBSM. General manager Bob Nims asked me to fill-in for vacationing John Parisi, their popular weekday morning meteorologist. What a way to finish my three year "career" at a radio station that was forever filling our kitchen with music, daily news, and weather ever since I could remember! It is a "swan song" week that holds a special corner in my heart.

My pre-sunrise walk from the dorm room to the top floor of the Lyndon State College student center where the meteorology lab was located is an indelible memory. Not only was it dark, still, and spooky, but the radiation fog that formed was so thick that the visibility made all of the campus buildings disappear. All I could see was the walkway directly in front of me. Even the campus lighting poles didn't come into view until I was within twenty or thirty feet. That fog was some of the thickest I would ever experience in my lifetime. Would some alien creature pop out of the fog to confront me? As silly as that may sound, it was a rogue thought that put a pep in my step. While it was disconcerting, I drew comfort in shifting my focus to drawing close to God in prayer. I knew that, despite the fog, He could see me, love me, and protect my steps. My sigh of relief was probably audible every time I saw the student center doors to begin my weather duties during my last week as a part of the WBSM family.

As a pilot, I'm not a fan of fog, but on quiet mornings at home, I embrace the fog and the sweet memories it brings to mind.

Tuesday, May 2, 2023
9:48 AM, Rain-Snow Mix, 34°F (1" On Deck)
Mile Marker 386

During my drive home from the station, I finished enjoying John Telich's podcast, Telich Talks. It was an episode that included the life story of Virgil Dominic from his own lips. Wow! So much I didn't know. Yet it was no surprise how God directed his steps in every season.

Virgil was often the news anchor fill-in on NBC's Today program. While the memory is but a fragment, I can remember seeing Virgil's news segments at the top and bottom of the hour whenever he filled in for Frank Blair, someone I remember with great clarity.

Before the era in which a separate personality had the duties of sharing national weather segments, I can still picture Frank's weather segments at the end of the news block. A national weather map was projected on a screen over his shoulder. I was intrigued with the projections and replicated them by drawing a national map with weather features backwards on a piece of paper, then examining them against the sun to make sure it all looked neat and correct.

This was in my elementary school years at then Mt. Pleasant Elementary school, less than a block away from our Sutton Street home (1966-1971). I remember bringing some of my "backwards map" artwork to school and showing them to a classmate,

Lorrie Barnes, who wanted to take them home and show her mother. She returned them shortly thereafter telling me that her mother was very impressed with my creativity, and that I would go far in my career as a media weather personality. I wish I knew where Lorrie was today so that I could thank her and her mother for one of the many encouragements that I received from my earliest recollections of wanting to do what Frank Blair did every morning on NBC's Today show.

Friday, May 5, 2023
8:54 AM, NACITS, Finally!, 50°F
Mile Marker 383

I woke several times last night and checked on the outdoor temperature to see a kinder, milder 50s°F. Doing that brings to mind a memory of seeing Dad always checking on the outdoor temperature anytime he got up in the middle of the night, sometimes using a flashlight to shine on the outdoor thermometer that was installed in the kitchen window. It's something he simply liked to know. In like fashion, like father, like son, I like to know what the atmosphere is doing even though I'll be returning to the world of sleep and dreams in the minutes that follow. Like so many other questions that have popped into my head since Dad's heavenly graduation in 2003, I'd love to ask him about this routine. Perhaps I would grasp onto why it is I like to do the same.

Friday, May 12, 2023
9:13 AM, Bright, Milky Sunshine, 66°F (Low: 48°F)
Mile Marker 376

How do I best foster a culture of team coaching? I can surely use a lesson from the man who hired me here in Cleveland: Virgil Dominic. He mentioned in a recent podcast with John Telich that he developed a style of never criticizing, but rather coaching people under his management care thanks to those who mentored him when he was a young radio and television news talent. (I wish I would have learned that much earlier in my career.) Mature people CAN learn new things! Hopefully, I can be an influence to encourage the forecasting philosophy that Dick Goddard started. It's a philosophy that I'm now responsible for passing on to my colleagues, a philosophy with which our audience related and gravitated. I truly want to see them succeed. Scott, Jenn, Dontae, Alexis, and Mackenzie are the best colleagues with whom I've had the pleasure of working! What a way to cap my television career. God is so good.

Monday, May 15, 2024
8:52 AM, NACITS, Dry, 55°F (Dew Point 31°F)
Mile Marker 372

Aside from waking my lifer friend, Pete, from jet lag sleep on Saturday evening (something for which I felt horrible because he dragged himself out of bed to chat with me), we had a great time catching up after his most recent cross-hemispheric cruise from

New Zealand to Hawaii. I needed to tell him the news of my pending retirement from television since it was wonderful heartfelt advice from Pete that helped me to properly assess life's journey in the proper perspective. This was something we started planning for long ago when Sally and I decided to aggressively seek to be debt-free, something we achieved in 1994 after many "peanut butter and jelly sandwiches." (We can thank Larry Burkett, founder of Christian Financial Concepts and a radio program called Money Matters for that!)

While the VHS videotape letters that Pete and I frequently exchanged for years eventually succumbed to technology, we used other means to stay close. Because Pete's perspective was so key in my decision to start a new life chapter, I refused to tell him via simple text or even phone call. It needed to be eyeball-to-eyeball, either by a quick flight to the "Minne-Apple" or by FaceTime. With less than eleven days remaining before I share it with my colleagues, it needed it to be sooner than later.

I'll be forever grateful for Pete's input. Watching him take his own advice over a decade ago added gravitas to a mindset that makes complete sense. I am fully persuaded that there will be no regrets and many amazing blessings that await us.

Thursday, May 18, 2023
9:54 AM, Sunny, 52°F (Dew Point = 33°F)
Mile Marker 369

I had another odd dream about returning to ParkTowne Apartments in Cedar Rapids last night. In the dream, I was moving into one of their newly built units, beautifully furnished, with a northern exposure out of the main windows. I don't know why I was there since WMT (KGAN) TV-2 did not seem to be in the dream at all.

For as little time as I was there in real life (roughly nine months, or less than 2% of my television career), Cedar Rapids and the Channel 2 family had a major impact on my life, probably because it was such a paradigm shift from the first 22 years of my life. Suddenly, I had to figure everything out on my own. Mom and Dad were over a thousand miles away. There was no "Facetime," texting, or even email for quick questions and replies. Thank goodness I paid attention when they tried teaching me important life skills. Three months into my new professional career, another strange sensation hit me. For the first time since kindergarten in September of 1964, there were no classes to rush to, no books to buy, no school clothes to prepare. As I mentioned in my first book, The Extra Mile, the only class of which I was a part was now the "working class." It was a period of time I dreamed about since elementary school days. Suddenly, I was standing in the middle of it all. Part of it was thrilling, but part of it was intimidating. Part of me embraced the world of independence, but a part of me yearned for the simplicity of my youthful dreaming days now behind me in the rear view mirror. It all happened far too quickly.

Monday, May 22, 2023
10:58 AM, Sunshine, 68°F (Dew Point = 45°F)
Washington Street Diner, Bainbridge, OH
Mile Marker 366

I just finished Chapter One of Frank Blair's autobiography as he described his last day of newscasting on NBC's Today program in 1975. My guess is that he was called to the Hebrews 12 mezzanine when I ordered his book. I told the Lord to let him know everything about me and that his book is a real comfort and template on how to approach and execute the final day of a long career. Now I'm looking forward to the remainder of the book and story.

When my media career started at WBSM in the summer of 1974 and then my commercial television career at WMT-2 in Iowa in May of 1981, envisioning the conclusion that is now one year from arriving was impossible. Even then, a long-tenure television career was not only difficult to complete, but I knew of so many whose "career" ended in disappointment and a change of careers for a variety of reasons. Yet, here I am almost thirty-five years after moving to Cleveland still at the same television station.

When I walk out the station doors a for the last time as an employee, I will have spent nineteen years on the weekday morning shift and eighteen years on weekdays prime-time, been through more news directors and general managers than I care to count, outlasting the on-air co-workers with whom I had the pleasure of working (...well, okay, most of them). Beyond trying to be conscientious in my daily tasks, I had little to do with my long tenure. There were many people with far more talent in the on-air performance realm. Only by the grace of God did I wiggle my way through the changing world of media in the now over a half-century of both television and radio. Beyond my role as an interim Pastor and itinerant evangelist, this is was what God designed me to do in my earthly journey. As I look back at how He sparked my interest in media meteorology, I'm amazed at how early he set my career path, and how much grace He had when I was actively looking for ways to go off course, something He did not let me do unless it would benefit me and my eventual destiny. Eventually, I'll get to a few of the detours that added depth and meaning to my journey from messy markers to digital doodles.

Wednesday, May 24, 2023
10:55 AM, Smokey Sun, 72°F (Dew Point = 56°F)
Mile Marker 364

Before leaving work yesterday, and with exactly 365 days remaining in this career chapter, I looked around. As much as we all loved Dick Goddard, I decided to make sure that I did not leave behind a mess of unwanted collectibles as I exited for the last time as an employee. We are still trying to weed all of that out years after his last day on FOX 8. I had to start somewhere.

That somewhere is where no one would draw early conclusions, my "utility/snack drawer" near the newsroom kitchenette. I aggressively tossed out quite a bit. I also put some of the items out on various counters where I knew someone would take it and use it. Two boxes of sanitary gloves leftover from the COVID "plandemic," a huge container of oatmeal, white spray paint used to paint one of the stones in the FOX 8 Front Yard weather set for white balancing, and a can of WD-40 (...I have NO IDEA why I had that in my drawer!). I brought home a box of FOX 8 business cards and a pair of perfectly new gardening gloves from my "TV8 Acres*" days, (*the twelve buy twelve foot television garden I had on the east side of the building in the 1990s). Now the drawer is half empty. The items that remained I may be using in the final year. It felt good to clean it out. It's a start.

Saturday, May 27, 2023
7:46 AM, NACITS, 45°F (Dew Point = 40°F)
Mile Marker 361

I wrote a long letter to (my sister) Ninette last weekend, including a first draft of the introduction of my memoir, <u>My Big Box Of Isobars</u>. I mentioned the erasable weather map she made me one year for Christmas when Tony was doing his medical residency in Burlington, Vermont. But when Tony was at Stonehill College a few years before (when Ninette and Tony were still dating), Tony mixed some calcium chloride solution for me in his college chemistry class. The solution, when painted and dried on anything, became a color-coded indicator of atmospheric moisture. Blue meant low humidity and sunny, dry weather. Purple meant change. Pink meant high humidity with rain in the forecast. White meant snow was coming.

I remember painting a dog's big eyes that Ninette drew on a piece of paper with the solution and hanging it on the front porch of the house in New Bedford. Watching the eyes change colors was spellbinding. I became excited when a weather forecast I announced based on its color changes came to pass. I was "hooked!"

As much as I would have loved the easy access to all kinds of weather data with just a few keystrokes on a home computer screen (still many decades away), the simplicity of weather observation with one's own eyes brought a level of direct involvement and subsequent excitement when it came to the atmosphere. This blessing may have been missed if my eyes were distracted and pressed into a computer display.

Tuesday, May 30, 2023
7:48 AM, Sunny, Hazy, 64°F (Dew Point = 55°F)
Mile Marker 358

One of the amazing stats about this May (2023) has been the amazing lack of severe weather, not only locally, but statewide. There hasn't been a single severe thunderstorm or tornado warning issued for the entire state of Ohio all month! I can't imagine that has ever happened in my lifetime.

Honestly, the quiet pattern has been welcoming... a real gift for me with 358 days remaining as a television meteorologist. I say that because severe weather television coverage has changed dramatically in the last few decades. In my summer in Iowa (1981), severe weather was not covered on live television, but we were required to break in to programming on WMT-620-AM. We had a microphone in the weather center wired into the AM radio board on the other side of the building. My heart raced every time I had to announce a new warning.

Fast-forward to my early years at WJW-TV. For the first five or so years (1988-1993), our severe weather coverage consisted of placing a "W" in the upper right corner of the television screen to alert viewers that a severe weather watch was in effect. Whenever a warning was issued, we would use a lower third crawl to dispense the information as quickly as possible. There was no easy way of breaking in live.

Sometime around 1993, we purchased an automated system to run severe weather crawls immediately. A television station in Oklahoma perfected and marketed the system that would push severe weather crawls to on-air in only a few seconds. It was a great system. Because we purchased a one-year exclusivity on "First Warning," we were the only station in Cleveland who could get warnings on-air within seconds of being issued.

Several years later, a competitor started breaking into programming for continuous coverage of any warnings, even fringe severe thunderstorm warnings. That opened up Pandora's Box. Suddenly, we were ALL "forced" to do the same. Ever since roughly 2000, anytime there is severe weather, especially tornado warnings, we are all continuously on-air. So what makes WJW-TV different? The dean of Cleveland weather Dick Goddard set our standard: We calmly disseminate the flow of information in a matter-of-fact, no-hype fashion. This saved my voice many times since going non-stop in any other fashion would tax my voice to the point of slipping out from under me when I needed it the most.

Covering severe weather was so taxing on all of us in the weather office that, when our son Noah was much younger, he added a nightly prayer during our family prayer time asking God to squelch any severe weather during periods when the threat was elevated.

With media delivery systems changing so much again, that routine will likely change past when this book goes to print. Will there be relief for media meteorologists looking forward? For my youthful colleagues that remain active in the business of television and internet news, I hope so. Perhaps this is a good use of AI.

Like several of my television mentors who have since retired (Barry Burbank, WBZ-TV, Boston; Paul Piorek, News 12 Long Island), I look forward to cozily watching weather drama unfold from my backyard deck or window just like I did as a young boy in New Bedford. That sure beats having my head buried in a array of Doppler radar monitors, unable to see the weather drama playing out with my own eyes.

Thursday, June 1, 2023
7:15 AM, NACITS, 54°F (Dew Point = 53°F)
Mile Marker 356

As I wrapped up my last on-air segment last night, I followed my routine of immediately walking over to the kitchen set where all of the wireless audio equipment is managed. I first unplug my IFB (audio receiver that allows producers to give the talent time cues and other info in that talent's ear) and return it to the bin. Next, I remove my wireless mic, but before I place it in the bin, I remove the piece of bright orange duck tape that holds the battery door shut while I'm wearing the mic. Duck tape, you ask? Yup. It has been a really low-tech solution to a high-tech problem.

All too often (before duck tape came to the rescue), the poorly designed battery door would quietly fling open from simple body movements, jogging from the front yard weather set to the studio one floor up. When my segment began and with the batteries on the floor somewhere in between the two locations, people at home couldn't hear me! My wireless mic was AWOL! It finally dawned on me that a simple piece of duck tape to secure the battery door would prevent the batteries from wiggling their way out of the transmitter on my belt. I use the same piece of bright orange tape for a few weeks until it stops feeling secure before replacing it with a new strip of duck tape.

Amazing... a multi-million dollar technical operation helped along by a three-inch piece of duck tape!

That got me thinking about other low-tech solutions that television news audiences never saw. The funniest on I can think of was from my first television weather job in Cedar Rapids, Iowa. WMT-TV-2 (now KGAN-TV-2) was one of the first stations in the country to use an 8-bit Hewlett-Packard computer to draw electronic weather maps.

We had to program it, line-by-line, in basic language. The hardware was in a standard electronics rack in the weather office across the hallway from the newsroom. The weather office, like most of the rest of the building, had industrial grade carpeting. In the winter, picking up static charges was easy. Discharges on doorknobs and the like were not a problem, but it your finger discharged on the rack mount holding the weather graphics computer or the Kavouras color radar display, the "fun" would begin. The radar display would stop working and any weather graphics you made would suddenly turn to a sea of digital gobbledegook. If that happened during a live weather segment (and it DID... way too often!), your ability to ad lib through a sea of digital nonsense was tested to the limit.

Chief meteorologist Dave Towne had the perfect (really low-tech) solution... a large plastic garden watering can. Every few days during the driest part of the winter season, Dave started watering the carpet in the weather office as if he was watering a newly planted garden. The moment anyone stepped into the weather office, any built-up static charge they may have been carrying was harmlessly discharged by the moisture in the carpet. Brilliant! Of course, we did have to deal with the musty odor of a damp carpet, but that was far better than having digital nonsense suddenly showing up on the "green screen" behind you. Once again, a multi-million dollar operation saved by a seventy-five cent plastic watering jug.

Monday, June 5, 2023
9:15 AM, Mostly Cloudy, 53°F (Dew Point = 45°F)
Mile Marker 352

It's difficult to wrap my head around the fact that, one year from now, I'll begin a new chapter. I think back to that first summer in Iowa, now forty-two years in the rearview mirror, and it doesn't seem possible that so much has happened in my profession. The saying, "the days are long but the years are short," holds a great deal of truth. So many special people from my summer in Iowa are no longer with us. Dear people like Lillian Bishop, my neighbor one floor below me at ParkTowne Apartments, and eternally youthful floor director and camera operator Peter Smith. I look forward to seeing both someday in heaven.

I'm eternally grateful to God that I have two deep friendships that remain to this day from my Iowa start. Then WMT-TV chief meteorologist Dave Towne along with a dear brother in the Lord (and in 1981, my competitor at KWWL-7 in Waterloo), Jeff "Kennedy" (Kronschnabel). Time has tested these two friendships and has found them solid, trustworthy, and essential (as iron sharpeneth iron).

Something that seemed to take forever to change were the "tally light butterflies," that is, that rush of adrenalin that suddenly made your heart race as each weather segment began. There were times when I wondered how many times my heart would put up with this. I also wondered if this anxiety, short of a panic attack, would ever stop. It never did in Iowa. How would I survive live, on-air segments on national television at <u>The Weather Channel</u>?

Oddly enough, I was more comfortable on national television (1982-1985) than I was back in local television at KARE-11 in Minneapolis (1985-1987)! It seemed as though the adrenalin always had a new surge waiting for me with every new career move.

It was only when I stopped thinking about it is when I started having fun with my co-workers. Now retired news anchor, Bill Martin, escorted me into this mindset without my even knowing it. Suddenly, the adrenalin rush was gone, replaced by a sense of supernatural joy and peace. There are those colleagues whom I envied because it seemed so natural from their first on-air segment. Why did it take over a decade for me to "settle down?"

It took more than two decades to see that heart-pumping, throat-drying adrenalin rush disappear during wall-to-wall tornado warning coverage, something I anticipated with dread during active severe weather outbreaks. Just ask my son Noah. As I alluded to earlier, Noah would often petition God for no severe weather when the potential was elevated during our family prayer time.

Thankfully, that anxiety slowly disappeared too. Nowadays, it helps to have a full weather staff to share any wall-to-wall severe weather coverage compared to the days when I was working solo with tornado sirens pushing my anxiety buttons.

My sense of feeling "alone" in my broadcast anxiety evaporated when I learned that I was not the only one who went through this. The first such revelation was listening to John Strossel share his struggle with on-air panic attacks during a segment on ABC's 20/20. What he described matched everything I had experienced! Then NBC's Today Show weatherman, Willard Scott, shared the same debilitating symptoms (his was an out-of-the-blue event that opened up a Pandora's box for him). Eventually, there were others that joined this group from former weather interns to co-workers to close friends. Even former teen idol, Donny Osmond, had to work through a season of crippling performance anxiety. I wish I would have known earlier.

All this to say that I am eternally grateful to God for escorting me through that valley to a land that is gloriously peaceful, joyful, and bright. Stepping off the platform of both local and national television with this peace is exactly where I hoped to be with that period now only 352 days away.

Friday, June 9, 2023
7:44 AM, Smokey Sun, 52°F (Dew Point = 51°F)
Mile Marker 348

I find it interesting that meteorology is expressed by numbers. Our atmosphere's motion (a fluid) can best be predicted by the laws of fluid dynamics, which are in turn expressed by equations. What gets plugged into equations? Numbers!

When I was still a toddler who spoke only French, well before my first day of kindergarten, I have distinct recollections of being absolutely fascinated with numbers. I couldn't get enough of them! In my mind, I can clearly see a little magnetic board that I had. It came with magnetic letters and numbers. I could care less about the letters. I used the numbers to digitally express the time (and that was way before digital clocks became popular) along with the current air temperature which was read on a dial thermometer in the east window of our kitchen. I would wait for the clock to show a different time or the thermometer to move up or down so that I could replace one of the numbers with another one. It entertained me for hours! I now wonder what was going on in my mother's mind as I was perfectly content to have fun with my magnetic numbers.

Fast forward a handful of years. Imagine my excitement to see digital LED watches comes in to fashion! You had to push a button on the watch's side to briefly illuminate the LED numeric expression of the current time. Because I used it constantly, I had to change the battery in it more often than most people.

When I was in middle school, WTEV-6, the CBS television station in our hometown of New Bedford, Massachusetts, started a promotion of giving away a countertop electric digital clock every hour if your name was selected from postcards sent in. You had to be watching at the top of every hour to see if your name was mentioned. If it was, you had a window of time to call and claim your free clock. Oh, how I wanted one of them! I sent in more than one postcard to increase my odds of having my name randomly pulled. I waited patiently all summer, faithfully tuning in at the top of every hour I could, but never heard my name. Those newfangled clocks were expensive, so I was not able to buy one. I had a manual wind-up Big Ben alarm clock that served me for years.

Nowadays, everything is digital! My home weather station. My clocks. My watch. Our thermostat. Our one lone battery operated back-up clock in the guest bathroom is the only analog time piece in our home. Periodically, I have to stop and remind myself of the days when I dreamed of digital equipment and it makes me smile. I can now actually thank God that I was not born into the "digital era." I may have taken it all for granted.

During the night, it's not unusual for me to wake up a few times during the night. As I mentioned before, my routine invariably includes a quick stop by my digital weather station display. It tells me everything I want to know without ever needing to step outside. While I don't need to know, it would seem strange not to check. It's how God wired me! It thrills me that He made me this way. Amen.

Sunday, June 11, 2023
7:27 AM, Lots Of Clouds, 62°F (Dew Point = 50°F)
Mile Marker 346

One of the many things for which I'm grateful to God is having been an active part of so many record weather events over my lifetime. No doubt, all in God's plan to fan the flames of my passion for meteorology.

One such event occurred on Saturday, August 2, 1975. I was 16-years-old and I can still recall (like it was yesterday) monitoring my Taylor Six's (U-tube Max-Min) thermometer. It was mounted on the shady sided of one of our porch pillars on the north side of my boyhood home in New Bedford, Massachusetts.

As temperatures rose above 100°F, I watched and marveled that our coastal New England city would be so hot. I also observed two other things that helped both my Six's thermometer and New Bedford Municipal Airport reach 107°F (an all-time New England record high temperature that still stands!). First was that the air was uncharacteristically "dry" (dew points were in the 50s). Second was the wind direction. It was from the northwest, not south or southwest. New Bedford saw the hottest temperature of anywhere in the northeast that day due to the maximum katabatic warming from the higher elevations northwest of New Bedford. What I saw on my Taylor Six's thermometer just before we left for church was exactly what New Bedford Airport (exactly one mile northwest of us) recorded, a temperature that has never been seen anywhere in New England since.

I still have that Six's thermometer. While it's in storage at the moment, I did employ it on the north side of our deck for a while. I also tried using it in Vermont (although I never found a place it would be safe). It followed me to Iowa (where it remained in storage), but did find a spot on my deck in Atlanta, Georgia (1982-1985). I can't remember if I found a place for it in Minneapolis (1985-1987). How it survived all those moves without being misplaced is beyond me, yet I am pleased that I still have it. It was a part of significant weather history. It took a lot of my newspaper route savings to buy it. The fact that I still have it is a testament to its use and wisdom in its purchase.

Sunday, June 18, 2023
7:58 AM, Hazy, Sun, 52°F (Morning LOW = 46°F)
Mile Marker 339

"Don't blink."

That's what Mom said when she thought about her life journey not long before she graduated to glory. I kind of got it when she said it, but as I prepare to lay aside a television career I strove to attain, I completely understand her admonition. Can it really be coming to a close? Only "yesterday," it seemed like our families were gathering together periodically at Burke Mountain, Vermont. Even before AirBnB existed, we rented one of several condos for extended weekends, mainly from mid-September to early October, and once in mid-December. Every single vacation was special in its own way. As recent as these Vermont adventures seem to be, the last big group family condo vacation was no later that 2002, over twenty years ago since Dad left us when he graduated to glory in December 2003. Needless to say, I miss them. Such gatherings in heaven will be far more amazing than the best vacation on this side of eternity. It escapes the wildest imagination! In due time.

Monday, June 19, 2023
7:29 AM, Clouds & Sun, 57°F (Dew Point = 52°F)
Mile Marker 338

Like any other work environment, having a group of committed people who have become more than workmates, more than friends, allows the workload to be light and the journey to be joyful and fun. I can say without reservation that the current weather office staff (Scott Sabol, Jenn Harcher, Dontaé Jones, Alexis Walters, Mackenzie Bart, and myself) is, by far, the best assembly that I have ever had the pleasure with whom to link arms. We all truly look out for one another. We have each other's backs. What a great way to navigate through my final year.

That hasn't always been the case. It would be easy to let the dust fly, but I would have to also admit that I've raised my own clouds of dust over the years. In every case, it was "dust" that should have been left unstirred. It's not an excuse, but stirring the dust is something anyone is more likely to do without maturity. Specifics would serve no purpose here, so why stir up dust that has long settled in the rear view mirror?

Wednesday, June 21, 2023
9:49 AM, Sunny, Warm, 73°F (Dew Point = 60°F)
Mile Marker 336

Over the decades, I've hosted some truly special guests on television. Some of the people that appeared with me on-air during weather segments included the hilarious Terry Bradshaw, Tim Conway (formerly a director at WJW-TV!), Tom Poston (from the TV sitcom Newhart), Scott's Baio (from Happy Days), along with Barry Williams and Maureen McCormick (Greg and Marcia Brady from The Brady Bunch).

But nothing compares to having my own father and mother appear with me at the "Coffee Quiz drum" to pull out a postcard for that Friday's Coffee Quiz during their first visit to Ohio in the summer of 1989.

Fast-forward to Monday, June 20, 2005. My first serious (high school) girlfriend Diane and her husband Paul had come to Cleveland to watch their Boston Red Sox play a three-game series with the Cleveland Indians. After finding out what hotel they were going to stay, I put together a fun "welcome basket" with tickets to a number of things that were on their Cleveland bucket list and had it delivered got their room ahead of their stay. That was fun enough... but I had one more pièce de résistance in my pocket.

I had Paul and Diane plan on coming to WJW-TV to "see the morning newscast" live. What they didn't know was my plan on having them actually ON the interview couch at the end of the three-hour morning block! News anchors Wayne Dawson and Tracy McCool had a blast asking Diane what I was like as a high school student. The segment is actually still on YouTube (just do a search for "Diane Gendron WJW").

After the newscast ended, I gave Paul the opportunity to jump into the chroma-key (green screen) and try his hand at a weather segment. This was a delight for me to arrange after hearing that, of all things, one of Paul's biggest hobbies is weather! His elaborate home weather station is a testimony to his interest. In fact, Paul shared with me that at one time he even entertained the idea of media meteorology as a career. What are the chances, right?

I am truly a blessed man to have had so many special people as my guest on-air with me over my career, but none more special than my parents and an amazing lifelong friend and her husband.

When Paul And Diane paid me a visit at the station, I remember asking God if He could bring Diane's mother to the viewing mezzanine (as laid out in Hebrews 12:1-2). A truly remarkable lady, she left

Earth and graduated to heaven far too early. I'm absolutely confident that she was watching the fun that we were all having that day, 18 years ago. It still makes me smile today, and always will.

Sunday, June 25, 2023
10:20 AM, Hazy Sunshine, 77°F (Dew Point = 66°F)
Mile Marker 332

Recently, the ABBA hit song Waterloo (from the summer of 1974) started playing in the car on my way home from work. It's a song that became one of my favorites. I was 15-years-old at the time. But every time the song plays somewhere, my mind "plays it" the way I heard it in 1974. Digital remastering makes it sound even better than it did in the original release, however, that's not how my mind plays it back.

Flashback: My brother Denié and our lifer friend from across the street, Jim Buckley, are enjoying a July summer afternoon on our front porch. Mom's favorite battery-operated AM radio at the time, a red Truetone DC3902 tabletop transistor radio, was tuned to 630-AM, WPRO, the Top 40 station out of Providence, Rhode Island. Because Waterloo was quickly rising in popularity, on its way to #6 on Billboard's Hot Singles chart in August, WPRO (and many other AM station) played it a lot.

Portable FM radios (like the FM radio stations that operated) were still a novelty and would not become popular for another few years. As a result, the clarity of AM radio reception was highly dependent on afternoon thunderstorms. Lightning discharges, even those a hundred miles away, began to cause the audio to "crackle." The more frequent and sharp the crackle, the closer the thunderstorm was. This phenomenon is called "sferics." It's the basis upon which the first crude lightning detectors were developed in the 1970s and 80s.

On this particular warm and humid summery afternoon, there must have been afternoon thunderstorms developing inland, away from the ocean breeze. As ABBA's song played, sferics added the foreboding sound of nearby lightning even though skies were filled with hazy sunshine.

Hearing the song Waterloo without the "snap, crackle, and pop" of sferics on AM radio somehow seems "all wrong!"

Whether I'm listening to ABBA's song via my Tesla's on-board Spotify account or on a TuneIn radio station (the most recent being KOKZ, appropriately enough in Waterloo, Iowa!), I'm forever transported to that carefree time of summer vacation from early high school, spending countless hours on our front porch with my brother Denié and next door neighbor friend Jim Buckley, feeling the freedom of summer and hearing the AM radio evidence of nearby thunderstorms.

Tuesday, June 27, 2023
6:26 AM, Rain Shower, 62°F (Dew Point = 62°)
Mile Markers 330

A thought hit me as I waited for one of my 6 PM weather segments last night. It echoes Don Kent's words to me when I interviewed him for WeatherJazz® almost two decades ago, but now I can make them mine: I surely have seen some dramatic changes in television weather segments in my career. For example, since moving to Cedar Rapids, Iowa for my first television weather job in the spring of 1981, the extended forecast page included an outlook for days number 3, 4, and 5. It was a very simple computer generated three-element bar graph with a single weather symbol to depict the overall weather condition of the day.

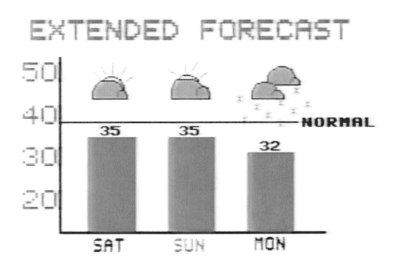

It was driven by one of my favorite forecast maps that came in via a "difax" printer twice a day, the 72-hour 500-millibar forecast map for the northern hemisphere. Short term was obviously important, but the challenge of trying to determine the weather on days number 3, 4, and 5 was exciting since it used analysis and forecasting skills based solely on the winds aloft chart.

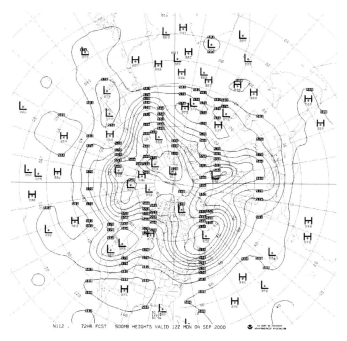

N112 . 72HR FCST   500MB HEIGHTS VALID 12Z MON 04 SEP 2000

Even if I tried to imagine it, I would have never fathomed a time in my career when the extended forecasts went much beyond this period. Any educated guess at days number 6 and beyond were impossible to predict with any kind of reasonable accuracy.

Fast forward to 2024. We have medium and long range forecast maps for ALL levels of the

atmosphere that extend out 120 to 240 hours...
some even beyond that! The kind of accuracy we
had on days number 4 and 5 back in 1981 is now
what we are seeing for days number 7, 8, 9, and 10!

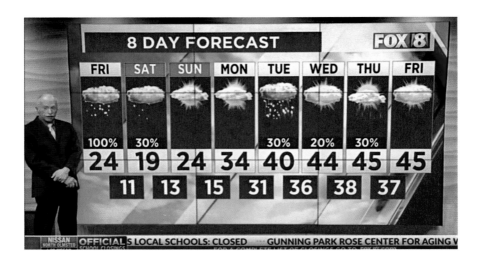

What will forecasts look like in a few more decades
and computer modeling speeds increase? I can't
even imagine! Perhaps in time, it will be
commonplace to see a 30-day outlook displayed by
media meteorologists. But how long will weather
segments need to be in order to do justice to
showing a 30-day outlook? We're fighting that now
with the FOX 8 Day Outlook, being constantly
reminded by FOX brass to spend enough time on the
8 Day Outlook so that our audience can assimilate
it.

Tuesday, July 5, 2023
10:07 AM, NACITS, 80°F (Dew Point = 69°F)
Mile Marker 322

I often marvel at all of the building modifications
that were done on my behalf to make our "Front
Yard Weather Set" possible. Everything we have
now can be traced back to an engineering staff that
was second to none. Led by chief engineer Mark
Thomas, the entire engineering crew, especially Jim
Snell, must have seen the vision I had to create a
weather set surrounded by a real world
atmosphere. News director turned general
manager Virgil Dominic gave our engineers the
tools they needed to use what we had to replicate
the outdoor weather set that Sally and I used at
KARE-TV-11 in Minneapolis in the mid 1980s. That
was no small task!

Jim Snell was able to locate an unused ENG (field)
camera to serve as the outdoor camera, but in order
to use chroma-key (also known as "green screen")
to project our weather graphics live from an
outdoor location, the camera needed to be modified.
The camera needed to be converted to send what is
called composite video into "RGB" video. It had
never been done using an old camera! Jim got
busy, excited to attempt something that had never
been done without buying a new and very
expensive camera.

A few months later, and after taking apart this well-
worn field camera, Jim rewired the camera to send
an "RGB" signal to the switcher up on the second

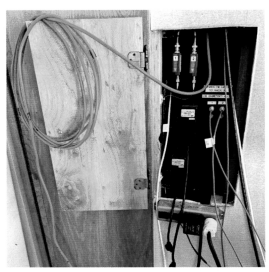

floor. But how? At the direction of chief engineer Mark Thomas, leave it to Jim and the rest of the engineering staff to start cutting the station's concrete and dry walls in order to "snake" the new RGB and audio lines from the vestibule at the station's front entry to the switcher on the opposite side of the building and one floor up! After a few weeks of fishing the lines from stud to stud, Jim was able to wire the new lines into the audio and video control switcher. But would it work? There was only one way to find out.

During the long break between the morning and noon newscast, I mounted a portable "green screen" (blue back in the early 1990s) outside the station's front door. The camera was fired up and pointed at the chroma-key screen. I stood in front of it, motioning to what would end up being our computer screen behind me and waited. What seemed like an hour passed by before Jim emerged from the front doors with one of the biggest, satisfying smiles I had ever seen. He did not need to tell me that our big experiment worked!

Eventually, after years of using old equipment and after many years of set-up and tear down, not only was a new digital RGB camera purchased, but it was mounted on a high-tech robotic camera so that it could be remotely operated by the studio robotics camera operator. The special metal-halide lamps that illuminated the outdoor set have since been replaced by efficient, high-output LED fixtures.

All of the persistence and dedication to creating a different visual experience for weather segments paid off. I thank God for the very small group (Virgil Dominic, Mark Thomas, Jim Snell, and a handful of others) who saw the potential despite the challenges. Those challenges were not exclusive to technology, but included others who could not get past "doing television" in a way that had never been done in Cleveland. It didn't take long for northeast Ohio viewers to embrace their television meteorologist presenting weather segments surrounded BY the real star, that is, the atmosphere! It was especially fun when the atmosphere was cantankerous, hitting me with wind-driven sleet and snow, or when not one but THREE waterspouts were dancing behind me during a live noon weather segment.

One of those concrete cutaways is still there, upgraded several times since that first time it was used to send a chroma-key video signal to a Grass Valley video switcher hundreds of feet away from our FOX 8 Front Yard Weather Set. I look at it and marvel, not at the technology it represents, but at the incredible people who got behind my hair-brained idea to make it work.

Tuesday, July 11, 2023
7:39 AM, NACITS, 60°F (Dew Point = 60°F)
Mile Marker 316

During one of my sessions working on my home deck installation, I had my Echo Dot outside with me so I could fill the air with music. I decided to listen to Classic American Top 40 ("the 70s"). Casey Kasem played a Number 1 song from the summer of 1975: "Love Will Keep Us Together" sung by The Captain and Tennille, a song written by Neil Sedaka. It stayed in the Billboard Number 1 position for an amazing four week run. This is how I remember that I had become a fixture at hometown station WBSM-1420AM in New Bedford, MA. (My first summer on-air was being a part of the Dick Stevens show doing the "boat and beach report" in the summer of 1974 between my freshman and sophomore year at New Bedford High School. I had just turned 15-years-old!)

By the summer of 1975, I was biking down to the WBSM studios on Pope's Island in New Bedford Harbor every single Saturday and Sunday morning before sunrise to record a 30-second forecast for news anchor Jim Philips. I did this for three years (as a volunteer without pay).

One certain Sunday morning, I arrived just as the Sunday morning disc jockey arrived. I can't remember his name, but I can picture him as clear as day: A young man about five-foot-ten with not-quite shoulder length scraggly red hair. For someone whose voice was medium timber and pitch, he actually had a good radio presence.

This particular Sunday must have been a rough one for him. Perhaps it was a late night up with friends or a date night. It was clear he desperately wanted a tall cup of strong coffee and a doughnut. He wondered if I would take control over the control board, run the network news, roll an "ID," and play a song or two while he ran across the street for a coffee and doughnut. I was thrilled to say yes! Imagine my euphoria of controlling what people in New Bedford were waking up to at just 16-years-old! I think that, technically at the time, not having a third-class FAA radiotelephone license, I should not have been given sole control, but the disc jockey was only going to be right across the street to get his coffee.

I asked him what songs he wanted me to play. He said, "Play what you want!" More euphoria!

Looking through the selection of songs on "cart" (they looked like 8-track tapes), and being a big fan of "top-40 radio," I picked the most uptempo song available to me: the Captain and Tennille's, Love Will Keep Us Together. For that short five or ten minute window, I changed the flavor of WBSM from your typical mom-and-pop mostly talk radio station to that of Providence's 92-PRO-FM or Boston's F-105. I had a blast and the morning jock was happy after returning with his tall coffee and a doughnut. No one ever knew, and until now, this story was quietly stored.

The Captain and Tennille's song is one of my favorites from the 1970s even without the covert Sunday morning programming personnel swap. Nonetheless, every time I hear that song, I can see WBSM's audio control board and how I woke New Bedford up one Sunday morning at 7 o'clock with that joyful, up beat tune.

Saturday, July 15, 2023
8:40 AM, Partly Cloudy, 73°F (Dew Point = 68°F)
Mile Marker 312

I've heard it said by others who have since retired from WJW-TV (like engineer Gary Jones, sports anchor John Telich, and news anchor Bill Martin): They never miss the daily grind, but they do miss the people.

Makes total sense.

That makes me think of everyone with whom I've had the privilege of working. At the risk of forgetting someone along the way, I'll cover that by introducing this as a "partial list." I cover many of these people in my first book every published called "The Extra Mile," a book still available on Amazon.

From WBSM, New Bedford (1974-1977): Dick Stevens, Jim Philips, Jim Loomis, Stan Lipp, Bob Nims, and Bill Brennan.

From WMT-TV (Cedar Rapids, Iowa) now KGAN-TV (1981-1982): Meteorologist Dave Towne, Lee

Dennis, news director Bob Jackson, anchors Gene Lively, Bob Brunner, Dave Shay, Maggie Jenson, studio crewman Peter Smith.

From The Weather Channel (1982-1985): Former professor turned co-founder of TWC Dr. Joe D'Aleo, John Coleman, Don Buser, Will Annen, Herb Stevens, and many former Lyndon State College classmates including Brian Durst (who recently went home to be with the Lord).

From Northwest Airlines in Minneapolis (1985-1987): Pete and Mindy Schenck, Robert "Van" Vannata, Bill Gough, and Scott Nickerson.

From KARE-TV-11 in Minneapolis (1985-1987): Chief meteorologist Paul Douglas, VP of news Tom Kirby, and director Frank Stackowitz.

From WJW-TV (1988-2024): Virgil Dominic, the legendary Dick Goddard, Mark Koontz, Neil Zurcher, Casey Coleman, Robin Swoboda, Wayne Dawson, Kelly O'Donnell (now at NBC News), Cal O'Kelly, Jim Snell, Don Quigley, Barry Zucherman, Gary Jones, AJ Colby, Jenn Harcher, Alexis Walters, Dontaé Jones, Mackenzie Bart, and so many others.

From WCRF-FM, Cleveland (1992-2015): Bob Devine, Dick Lee, Paul Carter, Gary Bittner, just to name a few.

And from (my current radio affiliation) WKJA, 91.9-FM, "Heartfelt Radio:" Mark Zimmerman,

Denise Pennington, Brian Brooks, and General Manager Mark Channon.

I'm certain that so many others will come to mind after I close this post. If you are reading this and we have had the pleasure of knowing each other or working with each other, smile to know that you have made my life abundantly rich.

I know full well that there are people yet in my future that will bring me much joy. I thank God, in advance, for you!

Wednesday, July 18, 2023
11:19 AM, Blue Skies, 75°F (Dew Point = 55°F)
Mile Marker 308

It has been almost one year (July 20, 2022) since I installed my Ambient weather station. I still marvel at the iPad app that gives me so much data. I can't even imagine how consumed I would have been when I was in elementary school, desiring as many "tools" for weather observation as possible. As primitive as many of my first instruments were, they were a source of unspeakable joy and hours upon hours of analysis.

When I was nine or ten years old, my parents bought me a weather observer's kit for Christmas. Part of the kit included a type of anemometer and wind vane that used a mechanical device attached to large, round pointers. Not instantaneous, it measured the average wind speed over a given time period (perhaps thirty seconds or so) while the wind direction was instantaneous. That device found a home on the corner of the vestibule which was visible from our south-facing kitchen window. I lamented that the device was too sheltered from the wind to be accurate, so my father offered to climb a very tall pole on our property to mount it higher so that I could see it catch the wind. While it was father away from the kitchen window, I could still read it.

Dad also did something I will forever remember. It was one of my early birthdays while I was in elementary school. Mom made me a birthday cake and gave me a few birthday gifts. Dad was working late at the restaurant so he arrived after Mom gave me my gifts and well after the cake was enjoyed. When Dad arrived home from work, he was carrying a bag from a store. He had one more gift to give me and he had no time to wrap it since he purchased it on his way home. It was a liquid-in-glass Tru-Temp outdoor thermometer with a special magnifying front that made its observation very easy. I was elated!

He told me that I could put that anywhere I wanted and that he would install it for me. Because I spent so much time in the bedroom I shared with my brother Denié, and because the window faced northwest and shaded from the effects of the sun from our neighbor's house, I chose that window. During a Saturday not long after he gifted me the thermometer, he took time that day to set up the ladder while I was inside showing him exactly where it was I wanted the thermometer. I'm sure it was an easy thing for him to do, but Dad never rushed me. It was a chance for him to fan the flames of a passion that I clearly had. I spent hours upon hours watching the temperature from that thermometer! (I found a photo of that vintage thermometer online recently and it made me smile!)

When I was in high school, my instruments began getting a bit more sophisticated. With my own money, I bought a Taylor Sixes thermometer from a downtown New Bedford nautical equipment store. (I made reference to that thermometer in an earlier post.)

I also purchased a Downeast anemometer and wind vane which was mounted on our cupola. The wired anemometer came into the same bedroom window where the Tru-Temp thermometer was mounted and whose two meters mounted on a finished wood block sat on the window sill. In my mind's ear, I can still hear that wind direction meter's needle bouncing back and forth when a warmer wind was bouncing between southeast (left) and southwest (right). After I graduated, I didn't have a place to mount it in my apartment in either Cedar Rapids or Atlanta, so I had Mom give it to my Uncle "Red" (George LeBlanc) who installed it on his oceanfront cottage on Sconticut Neck in Fairhaven where winds were not inhibited by houses.

As I approach the time in my life when I can spend a little more time with my eyes on the sky, I'm looking forward to regaining a sense of the wonder of our atmosphere. Not to say that somehow it was lost, but certainly with so much time spent in creating a weather story to which our television audience can fully relate, my fascination with weather has mostly gone dormant as required by my professional attention and duties. While I'm fully persuaded that it was God's designed destiny for me to fulfill, and while I would not have wanted my professional career to go any other way, I can appreciate the raw passion for weather observation that many others entertain.

For example, consider Paul Gendron, the husband of a wonderful, close longtime high school friend, Diane. While I did not meet Paul until they paid Cleveland a visit in June of 2005, Diane told me that Paul's love for weather runs deep. His New England home weather station is the envy of any weather enthusiast! Paul once told me that he wonders what it would have been like to follow that passion, making it a career choice. Yet I can point to innumerable times during the last half decade when I envied people like Paul who nurtured his passion for the weather by making its observation local and personal. You can call it a way of "staying in the moment," something to which I am truly looking forward post television.

Saturday, July 22, 2023
10:42 AM, Blue Skies, 72°F (Dew Point = 53°F)
Mile Marker 305

Like the last few mornings, I napped on the couch for a little while this morning after waking at 6 o'clock to watch the sunrise (and Bobby Conner on Elijah Streams). I noticed that sunrise is noticeably later than it was a month ago. Sunset and darker evening skies are also noticeably earlier, too.

I've been thinking much about God's assignment and destiny for me during my earthly journey. I discovered that assignment when I was a small boy. My deep-seated passion for weather went hand-in-hand with my fascination with numbers since fluids dynamics is easily expressed with many standard scientific equations. My desire to use whatever means I could to offer weather forecasts to the people around me often took creative twists. My biggest first break was when WBSM weekend radio host Dick Stevens allowed me to offer a quick "boat and beach report" to the radio audience. I had just turned 15 years old. In hindsight, I'm sure to Dick it was a "cute little segment" from someone whose voice still hadn't changed and lowered. What he didn't know was that once he opened that door, I wasn't going to let that door close at the end of the summer! WBSM could not get rid of me. I had been given great favor by the Lord and it was a part of my training for one of the purposes to which He gave me.

Radio and television was something I always viewed as "huge." I suppose that my view of these communication avenues was SO big, that it was intimidating. Once I broke into each estate, my heart would race every time I had a live segment to do. (I didn't get the same rush when I recorded segments since I knew that I could re-record them until I was satisfied with the result.) When I moved to Iowa in the summer of 1981 to start my first television job (at what was then WMT-TV-2, a CBS powerhouse affiliate), there were countless days when I wondered if I would ever see the day when my heart wouldn't race with an adrenaline rush when the red tally lights came on. To a limited degree, that anxiety settled down during my days at The Weather Channel (1982-1985) but it took more than a decade before I realized that I could truly "be myself" and have fun doing it.

Only once since knowing what my earthly assignment was did I take a short detour. Between The Weather Channel and my time at KARE-11 in Minneapolis, my career shifted. I was hired as a meteorologist by Northwest Airlines. I learned a ton about "upper-air meteorology," became close to many pilots and dispatchers, and enjoyed some great travel perks. All the while, there was a small unidentifiable gnawing sensation in my spirit. Eventually, several events drew my attention to the fact that I had stepped out of my God-given destiny and assignment. Nonetheless, God used my detour to place a wonderful lifer friend, Pete Schenck, and his family in our lives. God never wastes anything!

In 1988, we made our last move to back to Cleveland. That was 36 years a ago! Where did all that time go? There is so much truth in the saying that there are some days that never seem to end, but that the years zip past your eyes like a speeding bullet train.

Even so, the devil and his cohorts worked hard at derailing me from my destiny in ways I'd rather forget. The "grass is always greener" syndrome was often in play. Before our son Noah was born, I remember seriously looking at business properties in Lyndonville, Vermont, to open a McDonald's fast food franchise since my former college town didn't have one. It was a cash cow waiting for the right person. As great as the idea was, I also knew that it was a distraction that would take me away from my destiny.

As I approach the finish line of the television chapter of my assignment, I can look back and see what God was doing. He called me into the public eye so that He could minister to others through me. Like Jonah, I might have run in the opposite direction had He revealed that before its time. After four interim Pastoral commissions in northeast Ohio, I'm so grateful that God had an inordinate supply of patience in leading me through His plan.

Wednesday, August 2, 2023
1:26 PM, Smokey Sun, 77°F (Dew Point = 62°F)
Mile Marker 294

August is an interesting month for me. It was
almost always a month of preparation for things to
which I looked forward. While anticipating and
planning for (and dreaming about) the arrival of
autumn and winter in New Bedford was always on
my mind as a primary school student, the biggest
event was heading to Vermont for college.
Experiencing autumn foliage and early snows would
come much faster than in New Bedford, something I
could not wait to experience.

Nowadays, the same things come to mind, but for
different reasons. As a homeowner, summer
projects need to start wrapping up. The evening
sounds change from happy birdsongs to loud
cicadas and bullfrogs. A hint of fall foliage shows up
on any trees that are stressed. Sunsets are earlier
and can be noticed by August 1.

Unlike our newest meteorologist, Dontaé Jones
(who loves the heat and humidity of summer), the
cooler nights and drier dew point days are always
welcome for me. Nonetheless, now it's not without
at least a small measure of sadness that the long
days of summer are fading. It's a very reflective
month. I suppose it will always be that way, even
next August when a daily drive to 8500 Dick
Goddard Way will no longer be in my routine. I'll
keep a finger on the pulse of my spirit. If it is

different, I may be tempted to write yet another book!

Thursday, August 10, 2023
8:28 AM, Lots Of Clouds, 64°F (Dew Point = 63°F)
Mile Marker 286

Dave Stobbs stopped me in the FOX 8 hallway the other day. He told me that, in the process of weeding out old, outdated servers, he watched some "old" digital video files of our newscasts from 2012 when we had just moved from the SD (standard definition) world to HD (high definition). He commented that he saw so many people on-air that he did not recognize. He also mentioned that my hair hadn't yet turned gray.

I also remember it was a time when we still had to keep all the elements of the 8-day forecast inside the "SD" box since people who still had SD televisions complained that our 8-day forecasts were "cut off" the edges of the screen. It was an awkward time until we received the green light (about a year later) to operate in the HD (1280 by 720) space. Now that we've been HD for more than ten years, looking back at what the screen resolution looked like from the start of my professional career to now causes me to recoil! The screen looks small and perpetually out-of-focus compared to the crispness of HD. I find it fascinating that, so soon, I forget how enormous that change in television was! It's a very similar shift to the time we moved away from the WSR-57 ("old" non-Doppler NWS radar) to the WSR-88D NEXRAD Doppler radar in 1994. The contrast was stark and improvements unimaginable.

Once a routine has been established, it's easy to forget all of the quantum leaps that were taken to get to where we are today. Has it become information overload? While there is a danger of becoming too dependent on technology, the benefits seem to be outweighing the unique drawbacks. I wonder if Don Kent felt the same way about the advances he saw in the span of his career? I'd love to ask him that today. Don went home to be with the Lord only a few years after my WeatherJazz® interview with him in 2010. Don would have been 106-years-old today.

Thursday, August 24, 2023
9:16 AM, Drizzle, 66°F (Dew Point = 65°F)
Miler Marker 272

I'm trying to hunt down a photo that I'm sure exists somewhere in my digital files. It's a photo of the metal file cabinet near the entrance to my father's workshop at our childhood home in New Bedford, Massachusetts. I used it as a magnetic display panel on which I crafted weather forecasts. I did that using (bright green) magnetic letters that I purchased through the mail when I was in high school. If my memory serves me correctly, the company name was something like "Magna-Letters."

I knew about them since that's what WTEV-TV-6 in New Bedford used to display the weather forecast against a magnetic chromakey blue panel for Charlie Taylor's weekday evening forecasts on television. (I'll soon share more about some of the key moments that made my shadowing there so memorable.)

Back in the early 1970s, radio and television was the entirety of mass media. There were no other outlets. That remained until cable television started gaining ground in 1980 and satellite television soon thereafter.

Twenty years later, a new avenue for mass media developed when the internet began to slowly eat away at the "fourth estate" (traditional radio and television). Nowadays, the "fifth estate" is arguably becoming more prominent. Rumble (and other internet media outlets) are quickly becoming enormously popular. Tucker Carlson on "X" (formerly known as Twitter) and Dan Bongino's daily program on Rumble is doing what most mainstream media outlets is no longer doing, and that is to hold government officials accountable to "we the people." These outlets also offer everyday people to start their own "media channel." Young teens today have a new creative outlet to begin their broadcast careers. I often wonder what that would have looked like for me if I had been born in, say 2009. It will be fascinating to watch unfold even as I dabble in the fifth estate in the coming years.

Thursday, August 31, 2023
7:32 AM, NACITS, Cool, 50°F (Dew Point = 50°F)
Mile Marker 265

Today is the last day of (meteorological) summer. For the last handful of years, the autumn foliage was nowhere to be found on this date. Was this a trend? If so, it stopped this year. Pockets of autumnal color have been popping up over the last few weeks. As of yesterday (a VERY cool day with highs in the low 60s°F), there are some trees that are painted red and orange like they have been in mid-to-later September! It's actually good to see.

Post hurricane Idalia is now moving away from the Carolinas after hitting the panhandle of Florida as a CAT 3 yesterday. I'm letting things cool down on Instagram after starting a verbal firestorm several days ago when I pointed to the inappropriateness of referring to any hurricane as a "he" or "she." John Hope, former director of the National Hurricane Center and former Weather Channel colleague from the 1980s made it a point to remind all on and off air meteorologists that a hurricane was not a living thing. Thankfully, some level-headed people came to my rescue, but there were too many that thought my post was ridiculous and worse. As rude and insulting as some of the comments were, I did my best to exercise restraint. I can still hear my mother's voice when I was learning how to drive and a crazy driver was testing my skill and patience.

"Give them the road," she exclaimed, "just give them the road!"

That little bit of advice has served me well on the road over the decades, and it served me well in the social media world as well. But what it doesn't help with is the realization that we are all surrounded by the kind of people that seem to enjoy trying to spread their own misery, nonsense, and worse. Sometimes deciding not to get drawn into an endless loop of verbal sparring is not very satisfying, but in the end it will save me from having to deal with needless excess adrenalin.

On this side of eternity, we will all have to deal with miserable people and malcontents, but I'm looking forward to navigating those intersections with far less frequency as I step off the public stage. It's my desire to leave a trail of faith, hope, and love wherever I leave my physical and digital footprints.

Monday, September 11, 2023
10:04 AM, Partly Cloudy, 65°F
Mile Marker 254

Thank you, Sweetwater, for carrying such a huge array of handpans! I came home with one and will now search for a good handpan online instructor.

Now that we are seeing the leaves changing and the weather cooling, I find myself wondering what summer 2024 will be like after a full season retired from television. For starters, I'm committed to starting a raised bed garden in 2024. With more time to attend to a garden, produce will be organic and without chemical assistance next summer. Some of my inspiration comes from watching Neil Manausa expand his garden in northern Virginia over the last few years.

I'm also seeing the need to connect to my heavenly Father through prayer on a much more intentional scale. Prayer walks down Beechwood Drive will be the start of it.

Tuesday, September 12, 2023
8:34 AM, Dark Overcast, 62°F
Mile Marker 253

I've been wondering where I should go next in my career recollections. Honestly, I've hit a bit of a pause point. I've spent a good deal of time recalling some of the foundational moments that established my journey in this sometimes crazy business. I suppose those foundational moments needed to be painted first before I spent any time on the highlights of my time in Cleveland. Once more, I think of television painter Bob Ross telling me to lay down the background and landscape before I attempt to add the finer details of objects in the foreground. Now that I have painted a good deal of that landscape (although I am not totally done with it), I may soon begin to add some of what made my ride at WJW-TV so amazing.

Friday, September 22, 2023
8:36 AM, Milky Sun, 57°F (Morning Low = 55°F)
Mile Marker 243

So how does my WJW-TV story begin? It begins long before January 1981, just before the launch of Cleveland's very first legitimate weekday morning newscast. That thread needs to go back to the early 1980s when I was at The Weather Channel in Atlanta.

During that time, I somehow heard that Cleveland weather legend Dick Goddard was a huge TWC fan, so when The Weather Channel had enough people to start its own bowling league, I formed a team with Sally, Brian Durst (now enjoying heavenly bowling leagues), and a young lady from the art department whose name now escapes me. I suggested calling ourselves The Woollybear Watchers. I wrote to Dick Goddard asking if he had any woollybear paraphernalia that we could use. It wasn't long before a package arrived with woollybear t-shirts for everyone and all kinds of woollybear gear. I mailed Dick photos of our team highlighting his t-shirts. Little did I know that it would start a long friendship that would pave the way to WJW-TV a half-decade later.

Fast-forward to December 1987. I had given up my career in aviation meteorology at Northwest Airline on September 1st to return to television weather full-time, joining my wife Sally at the NBC affiliate, KARE-11. While I was full-time at KARE-11, I was not (yet) under contract, so when Sally's mother called us one day when we were finishing our day in the KARE-11 weather office, everything "clicked." Sally's mother read us an article in the Cleveland Plain Dealer about WJW's plans to start a new morning show. The article elaborated about how all of the pieces of the puzzle were in place except for one. They were still looking for a meteorologist. That's why Sally's mother called.

I looked at Sally and asked her if she wanted to "head back home." I remember no hesitation at her affirmative reply.

I began preparing my resumé and videotape and called Dick Goddard that afternoon.

"Hi Dick! I understand you're still looking for a weekday morning meteorologist. If I overnighted a tape and resume to you, would you be willing to carry it into your news director's office with an introduction and endorsement?"

Dick was more than pleased to be my conduit! I dropped off my package at the Wayzata, Minnesota post office with postal clerk George Kroeck, someone who saw me mailing resumé tapes often since September. As I wrote about in my book, The Extra Mile, I sensed that George knew that this package was different. This was the one that would open a gateway from Minneapolis to, in this case, Cleveland. George was right.

Only eight days later (interesting number given that WJW-TV is Channel 8), I was at WJW-TV for an interview. By mid-afternoon, news director Virgil

Dominic and general manager David Whitaker gifted me with an offer that I could not refuse. They encouraged me to call Sally to let her know that we were coming home.

Christmas and New Year's Day flew by that year. Only a few days past January 1, 1987, I started my solo drive to Ohio to begin planting roots while Sally put our Minnesota house up for sale. KARE-11 brass was exceedingly gracious and kind, telling us that as soon as our Minnesota house sold, they would release Sally from her contract early so that she could join me in Ohio.

While our morning newscast debuted in early February of 1987, WJW-TV allowed me to fly up to Minnesota in July to join Sally on her last weekday morning newscast joined by two of our dearest lifer friends, Pete and Mindy Schenck and their two very young daughters Carrie and Janet (who made a cameo appearance in the "News-11 Backyard" outdoor weather set with me).

Now, in hindsight, I can see God's gracious Hand in patiently putting all of the pieces of the puzzle together in a way that took more than five years to unfold and in ways that I could never fathom.

Monday, October 2, 2023
10:07 AM, NACITS, 65°F
Mile Marker 233

October. One of my favorite months. Peak fall
foliage. Cool nights. Pumpkin beer from western
New York. I used to really like the earlier sunsets. I
still do, but it is mixed with a melancholy of sorts,
especially in the morning when I wander into the
kitchen in total darkness.

Time seems to be accelerating toward "Mile Marker
Zero." I'm glad I've started arranging things that
need attention now, not waiting to the last minute
to account for unforeseen challenges.

I've begun giving executive producer Chris Gibilisco
a list of special people from whom I would love to
see a short congratulatory video during next May's
monthlong send off. The first on my short list was
Iceland's pop artist Jón Jónsson, an inspiring
family man whose music is simply
"framúrskarandi" (on of my favorite Icelandic
words that means outstanding). He was a special
guest on an episode of WeatherJazz® and has been a
delightful friend ever since.

Second on my list is Jeff "Kennedy," someone who
was my direct competition at my first television job
in Iowa in the summer of 1981. Jeff was on
KWWL-7 (the NBC affiliate) and I was at WMT-2
(the CBS affiliate). We never communicated with
each other in 1981 since friendships with your
competition was something that was largely

frowned upon at that time. We began communicating with each other years after I moved to Cleveland and discovered that he almost moved to WOIO-19. It was only then we discovered that we had a similar faith journey. In hindsight, I wish we had fostered a friendship when I lived in Iowa, but I'm eternally grateful for that friendship now.

There will be plenty more along with what will be a number of surprises, I'm sure. May 2024 will be here before I know it.

Wednesday, October 11, 2023
9:45 AM, Variable Clouds & Sun, 48°F
Mile Marker 224
Fall Foliage 43%

On the mend after a couple of challenging days. Two days ago, the December Iceland trip was only an idea. As of last night, (first class) airfare, Seltjarnarnes AirBnB, Avis car rental, and (four) Jón Jónsson (IceGuys) concert tickets purchased. Bob Gilmore is making the trip with me! It was this same Bob who adventurously agreed to come with me for a three-day Iceland discovery trip in March of 1987. Here we are, almost four decades later, doing it again, except this time we have a ton of friends who live in Iceland to see! (Our visit and the concert will be a complete surprise for Gunnar Gunnarsson. HA!) Will this be my last trip to Iceland? Probably, but who knows?

There were no newscasts at 4 PM, 5 PM, 6 PM, or 7 PM last night due to MLB baseball. I felt well enough to show up and socialize for a while, something none of us can do very easily during a normal workday. It was nice just sitting down and shooting the breeze with Dontaé and Mackenzie.

Our staff is quite large compared to my early days at WJW when we had only three of us total (Dick Goddard, Mark Koontz, and me). Because of our newscast schedule, we somewhat easily relied on each other to fill all the gaps when we went on vacation. Nowadays, with more than half the day occupied by live, local news and weather, our weather staff has grown to six.

When I signed my last contract in January 2023, I had a wonderful conversation with our general manager Paul Perozini. I wanted to tell him just how grateful I was that WJW took the time needed to hire the right people in the last few years. I'm not exaggerating when I say that our current crew is the best one with whom I've ever had the privilege to work. For the first time in my career, every single meteorologist honestly cares for and looks out for everyone else in ways I have never seen. It almost tempts me to stay on for another few years to enjoy this most unusual camaraderie.

Usually in local television, egos and self-aggrandizing attitudes can complicate relationships. As a follower of Christ, I've attempted to prevent these attributes from creeping into my own persona. Sometimes in this business, it's a tall order. Meandering down into that rabbit hole would take another separate book (or two, or three!). That kind of book material would be strangely absent if one relied on spending time with our current crew (Scott Sabol, Jenn Harcher, Alexis Walters, Dontaé Jones, Mackenzie Bart, and myself). It's like having the best dessert ever at the end of a long and complex meal. I'm at blessed man to have such great co-workers surrounding me as I pass along my big box of television isobars.

Thursday, October 26, 2023
9:36 AM, A Mackerel Sky, 63°F
Mike Marker 209

Dontaé, Mackenzie, and I were laughing hysterically about some of the funny things that have happened to us over the years in television and radio. This is probably a good place in My Big Box Of Isobars to spend some time laughing as the mile markers zip by.

I can still hear Dontaé laughing at my story from my college radio days at WWLR-FM. The station used to air the Lyndon State Hornets basketball games when they played at home. This is where the fun began.

One day, I was asked if I would pinch-hit as the "color commentator" since that person was unavailable for the broadcast. I resisted, never having done "color" for any sporting event before.

Besides, I was not overly familiar with the nuances of basketball. I was assured that it was easy. After several declines, and after being relentlessly strong armed, I finally (reluctantly) agreed.

Fast-forward to the gymnasium. The play-by-play announcer and I settled into our press box seats. Unceremoniously, the game began. The play-by-play announcer was good. I chimed in wherever I could but my contributions felt less than amateurish.

About ten minutes after the game began, one of the radio station engineers arrived and approached the radio booth. He waved at us and gave us the "cut" signal across his throat. We looked at him quizzically.

"You're off the air," he said.

Initially, we thought there was a technical problem.

"Is there a technical issue," we asked?

"Nope. The general manager was listening and he thought (André) was SO bad that he ordered that the plug be pulled. Don't worry. We made it sound as if the issue was technical."

It's not like I didn't try to warn them. Despite that, it was still my hope that I could have done a reasonable job. Embarrassed? Sure. But aside from the college radio colleagues, no one ever found out that our live coverage stopped because of my performance.

Lesson learned: Stick to something you know intimately. Weather!

Thursday, November 2, 2023
8:16 AM, Cloudy, 33°F (Trace of Snow Remains)
Mile Marker 202

We had 2" of snow fall early Wednesday morning... hello, November! Much of it stayed on the ground as highs stayed in the 30s°F. It will disappear today, to return sooner than later.

Bill Martin was right. When I first started the mile marker countdown, it was just under 500 days. These next 200-or-so days will fly far faster than the most recent 200.

Saturday, November 11, 2023
8:40 AM, Overcast with Bright Spots, 41°F
Mile Marker 193

When I started the Cleveland chapter of my career in 1988 at age 28, while technology had advanced considerably since starting my professional career in Cedar Rapids in 1981, we still did not have home internet connections or cell phones. We relied on information received from radio and television newscasts at prescribed times, so examining real-time data was limited to whatever you could see with your eyes in your location.

I can vividly recall my early morning departure sequence from home at 3 o'clock in the morning. We were forecasting some lake effect snow squalls the day before. I watched the occasional snow showers visit our Geauga County backyard while I ate breakfast at 2 AM and knew my drive into work would be a little gnarly, but little did I know what awaited me as I gulped my first cup of coffee with whatever it was I had for breakfast.

There was nothing out of the ordinary during my 3 AM departure. As I opened the garage door, I took a moment to watch the sincere snow shower falling against our security light over the garage. I did not waste much time as I knew my drive into work would take longer than the customary 30 minutes.

By the time I backed out from the driveway, the snow shower went from sincere to supreme. It seemed like a new inch of snow had fallen in less than a minute. Slowly, I crawled to the stop sign at the main road. By that time, I could barely see the stop sign and it was right in front of me! I could not see where the road was. I could not see where the ditch was. I couldn't even see where the other side of the main street was. I looked all around me and all I could see was a windswept swirl of snowflakes so heavy, that I honestly couldn't see anything else. Panic swept over me. Would this follow me to the station? Was this an isolated super-squall out of which I would drive in a block or two? I waited. One minute, then two. No change. There is absolutely no way I could proceed safely.

Slowly, I returned to the safety of our garage and walked back into the house to call the newsroom managers. I let them know that I would be delayed as long as the snow was reducing visibility to near-zero. I was happy to hear that the snow was very light in Cleveland proper, but without seeing the radar returns from Cleveland, I had no way of knowing when our snow blitz would abate.

While I was on the phone with our managers, I noticed that the snow eased up a little. I told them that I would give it another try and quickly crawled back in to my vehicle. This time, I could see the freshly coated road at the stop sign. The roads were very slippery with the freshly-fallen, unplowed snow, but I could at least see where the road was.

I encountered a handful of heavier snow showers on the drive in to the station, but nothing that came close to the visibility-stealing super-squall that stopped me dead in my tracks just minutes before. It was the heaviest fall of snow I ever experienced, unequalled by anything since in over thirty years of commuting!

Nowadays, I might instantly pull up the high-resolution NEXRAD radar loop thanks to fiber-optics internet to "see" how long I would have to wait before I had a departure window that was drivable. These are awesome tools to have. I suspect we have become so used to this amazing information stream that, in the event of an "internet blackout," almost everyone would be paralyzed by it!

Thursday, November 30, 2023
10:05 AM, Bright, Milky Sun, 40°F (2" On Ground)
Mile Marker 174

What a challenging Tuesday. At 4 AM, there was no snow on the ground. When I woke at 6 AM, there was easily 6" of new, fluffy, wind blown snow. With an Amazon delivery only 2 stops away, I quickly donned a winter coat, a Mad Bomber hat, gloves, and ski pants over my pajamas to clear the snow with the snow blower (prepped the night before). The delivery never came that morning. *sigh* Then it was off to officiate Jim Snell's funeral in Vermilion, a drive that took nearly 3 hours, witnessing the aftermath of no less than two dozen spin outs and accidents along the way.

God was honored. I also spoke with one of Jim's WBNO colleagues, a bi-vocational pastor who asked Jim if he was "a believer," to which he responded, "yes!" Confirmation!

I wrote about Jim's amazing talent earlier when he converted an ENG camera into an RGB camera. When I wrote that portion of this book, I was looking forward to sending him a copy so he could see his name in print. Now I'll need to send him a heavenly copy.

Monday, December 4, 2023
11:40 AM, Thick Overcast, 37°F
Mile Marker 170

As I approach the day when I started my "mile marker" journey at "495" (January 13, 2024), I seemed to have hit a period of time where I've been reflecting on the people who have transitioned beyond the eternal curtain and how many of them invested in me in ways I had not considered until recently. People who treated me with simple kindness like "Wally," an engineer from WMT-2 (now KGAN-2), Cedar Rapids, Iowa, and another master control operator-engineer, Cal O'Kelly, from my early years at WJW-TV. So many others from The Weather Channel (Atlanta) and KARE-11 and Northwest Airline (Minneapolis) years that fill the space in between my humble start and now. Each have filled my journey with an important piece of life's tapestry. I'm a bit melancholy that I'm not able to thank them properly for their role in my career journey. I'm hopeful that each will receive a copy of this book in heaven as an expression of my gratitude for walking alongside me with kind words and encouragement at key moments in my career. In many cases, they are key moments that I have come to recognize only well after each occurred. My only wish here is that I would have realized earlier just how important each person was in my sojourn.

There are simply too many to name here. I ask the Spirit of God to deliver a copy of this book to each person who exercised even the smallest courtesy of kindness to me, especially to those I tried to earnestly to locate but was unable. With my hands clasped together in reverence, Lord, I thank you from the bottom of my heart.

Tuesday, December 19, 2023
Seltjarnarnes, ICELAND
3:50 AM GMT, Cloudy, 34°F
Mile Marker 155

The Grindavik volcano has erupted. It began about four hours ago. The lava crack is 4 km north of Grindavik not far from the Blue Lagoon.

This was the news that greeted us when we woke to make our final prep and clean up to fly home at 10 o'clock (Iceland Time) today. I'm certain we will see the glow from the eruption from Route 41 between Reykjavik and Keflavik.

Monday, Christmas Day, December 25, 2023
8:56 AM, Cloudy, Mild, 47°F (No Snow Remains)
Mile Marker 149

Despite being delayed by one day due to 60-80 m.p.h. winds, my Iceland adventure with Bob Gilmore was nothing short of amazing. To think that this trip may be a bookend to the first adventure we took back in March of 1987 makes me smile with satisfaction.

There were SO MANY amazing highlights not the least of which was driving past fountains and rivers of lava near the intersection of Route 41 and Route 43 on the way to Keflavik Airport during the eruption that started at 10 PM the night before (as we slept!). Bob took video of the eruption outside our Land Rover as I drove to the airport. Bob then uploaded the video in 4K so that FOX 8 could download it and use it as a "local angle" to a world news story... which everyone at FOX 8 loved! Talk about being in the right place at the right time!

Jón Jónsson and the IceGuys concert was worth all of the planning. It is arguably one of the most amazing concerts I have ever attended... yes, even better than the Queen concert I went to in 1976 with many high school friends. As busy as Jón was preparing, I still received a text message wondering if we had made it to Kaplakriki (the concert venue)!

During our live radio interview (totally unexpected!) at FM95.7 with the morning crew (Rikki, Egill, and Kristin), they confirmed what I already knew... that Jón is a genuinely generous and caring man who loves his family and friends deeply. It's no surprise that they all revered Jón and his music.

Our visit to RÚV was great fun. Darren Adam not only took care of us well, but interviewed Bob and me for his program, the RÚV English Radio Program (which aired on Tuesday, December 19, the day we flew back home).

Our upgraded (diesel) Land Rover was perfect since the weather was quite dicey at times with snow and ice. The driveway of our Seltjarnarnes AirBnB apartment on Melabraut was totally covered with glaze ice on our final full day. Navigating our way from the Land Rover to the apartment's front door was quite an adventure after dinner! Our hiking shoes were useless. We would have been better off with a pair of ice skates!

Flying first class in both directions was an amazing experience on Icelandair. Seeing the northern lights from 41,000 feet on the way TO Reykjavik was a real treat!

With a long Christmas vacation (I don't return to FOX 8 until January 2, 2024), the week ahead looks peaceful. I thought about Christmases past when I would often spend more than an hour on the phone with Mom and Dad. Even though it has been twenty-one Christmases without Dad and fourteen without Mom, I still miss them terribly... but I wouldn't want them to return to this often troubled, sin-marred world. I'm fully persuaded that Christmases in heaven with Jesus are indescribable. Praise God Jesus accepted the rescue plan that God the Father had in mind. That's why we celebrate... the coming of our Savior.

Thursday, December 28, 2023
9:18 AM, Rain, 44°F (No Snow OG)
Mile Marker 146

When last night's dense fog obscured the neighborhood, I stood at the edge of the driveway for a moment after wheeling the trash bin out and just absorbed the intense quiet. That's when I realized just how infrequently we are visited by pea soup fog compared to my boyhood days in coastal New England.

I already wrote about some of the intensely foggy mornings I experienced in my younger days in the northeast, but this recollection was more of a synoptic assessment. Since very thick dense fog is more uncommon here in Ohio by-in-large, I tend to appreciate what comes with it: air that is SO still and quiet that it's almost unnerving! You hear your own breathing and heartbeat. Your thoughts become the only thing you "hear." All the better if they are peaceful, joyful thoughts.

After deeply drinking in the scene for myself, I ran back in the house to grab my smartphone to snap a few creative photos.

Top Left: 5th Grade Photo - 1960
Top Right: College TV Weather Set Lyndon State
College, Lyndonville, VT 1980

Above: The Weather Channel, Atlanta, 1983.

Right: TV Guide
Promo, Iowa, 1981

Top: WJW-TV from
Cleveland's record
cold day (-20°F)
January 19, 1994

Saturday
8 PM to 10:20 PM

⑤⑤⑥⑨⑩ LOVE BOAT (CC)
1. April the nanny (Charo) and her charges fail to debark before sailing. 2. A young man (Michael Lembeck) puts on officious airs for his boss (Ralph Bellamy), but plays it cool for the boss's antiestablishment daughter (Laurette Spang). 3. A young man (Vincent Van Patten) falls for his best friend's mother (Samantha Eggar). Gopher: Fred Grandy. Captain: Gavin MacLeod. Doc: Bernie Kopell. Isaac: Ted Lange. (Repeat; 60 min.)
Additional Cast
Ty Younger .... Larry Linville
Lisa .... Tasha Martell
Billy .... Philip Brown
⑥⑦⑬ BJ AND THE BEAR
A bumbling but tenacious police detective suspects insurance fraud when a valuable painting is stolen from BJ's office. BJ: Greg Evigan. Callie: Linda McCullough. Stacks: Judy Landers. Cindy: Sherilyn Wolter. Grant: Murray Hamilton. (Repeat; 60 min.)
Guest Cast
Detective Finger ...... Greg Mullavey

JULY 25, 1981
PRIME-TIME CHART IS ON A-15

Sergeant Williams ...... Paul Tulley
Stella .... Donna Theodore
Captain Dryer .... Jack Kelly
Mose .... Peter Lupus
Nick .... John Dullaghan
⑨Ⓒ PRINCE AND HIS LADY: WEDDING OF THE CENTURY
Special: A report on the pageantry and history of the British Royal Family. Included in the preview are visits to the bride's dress designer and the royal baker; interviews with Scotland Yard officials about security for the wedding; and films of historic events in the British Empire. (60 min.)
[Pre-empts regular programming.]
⑪⑫㉑㉜ MOVIE—Musical
"Mother Wore Tights." (1947) The ups and downs of a vaudeville team (Betty Grable, Dan Dailey). Iris: Mona Freeman. (2 hrs.)
㉛ NASL SOCCER
The Edmonton Drillers take on the Roughnecks at Tulsa, Okla. (Live)
⑧⑤ MOVIE—Thriller
"The Awakening." (1980) R: Violence. An archaeologist (Charlton Heston)

WJW Studio
July 4, 2020

Summiting a Vermont peak near Killington 1995.

Bill Martin cuts André's tie off on live TV.

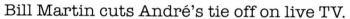

Dick Goddard on his last on-air day, November 22, 2016.

Trying some of my Icelandic on FM 95.7 in Reykjavik, Iceland
on Iceland's most popular morning radio program called Brennslan
(means "The Burning") in mid-December 2023.

My last evening on-air surrounded by longtime friends
from Virginia (Neil and Dawn Manausa left,
Kevin Kennedy right).

Tending to my new raised bed garden post retirement.

2024

Monday, January 1, 2024
11:42 AM, Snow Showers, 32°F (Lawn Dusting)
Mile Marker 142

Everything will start to go quickly now. There is so much that needs attention before May arrives. My memory of preparing to leave Cedar Rapids for Atlanta at the end of February 1982 is sketchy, but I do remember being both excited and a little overwhelmed with the loose ends that needed closing. More than anything, I still remember with great clarity putting Iowa in the rear view mirror and all of the adrenalin induced sensations that accompanied the first leg of my drive to Atlanta.

When I finally stopped for the night in Vincennes, Indiana, it was windy, cold, and dark. That only served to add to the second-guessing of making such a major shift. Arriving at my new apartment (then Woodchase Apartments in Marietta, Georgia) is also something I remember with stunning clarity. It was cloudy, rainy, cold, and somewhat dark when I opened the door to 1000-C Woodchase Lane. The apartment was cold, dark, and empty. I was quick to turn on lights and turn on the heat just to change the scene. Within an hour, optimism finally began to bubble up.

Trying to get a sense of what it will be like waking up Thursday morning, May 23rd is an exercise in futility. I'm sure there will be a plethora of emotions that will drive the boat, but until I get there, I won't know how to best navigate those waters. I will trust God as He supplies what I need.

Thursday, January 4, 2024
10:15 AM, Cloudy, Cold, 27°F (1" New Snow)
Mile Marker 139

At the Costco checkout this evening, I ran into
Anita. She recalled a story of meeting me years ago
at the grand opening of Cleveland's Galleria where
we nearly collided. She was so joyful and upbeat
that it was impossible not to smile and laugh as we
exchanged pleasantries. She made my evening. On
the way home, the Lord accented what I thought
about on the way home. My successful television
career was not about me at all (something I
fortunately learned early). It was about bringing
joy to those who tuned in, not only for a weather
forecast but, for a momentary smile that might not
have otherwise occurred that day. Just like Bill
Martin used to say, "If I'm able to make someone
smile or laugh in the course of a newscast, then I've
done my job." Amen.

Monday, January 8, 2024
8:46 AM, Overcast, 31°F (1/2" OG)
Mile Marker 135

I thought for certain I wrote about an anticipated
Iowa ground-blizzard that never happened, but that
isn't the case. Leaving this event out of my swan-
song book would be like having a noticeable empty
swath visible on a near-completed painting! Let's
fill in that swath before it escapes me again.

Dateline: Friday, January 22, 1982. I had already announced to my boss, Bob Jackson, that I accepted the job offer at The Weather Channel and that my last day would be Friday, February 26. A deepening storm was headed for the midwest. In its wake, ground blizzards were expected in Iowa Friday night and early Saturday morning. The ground blizzard warnings got Bob Jackson's attention. Suddenly, a grand plan to cover the impending blizzard was hatched. Bob told us that between Dave Towne and me, we would track the ground blizzard around the clock, every half-hour with cut-ins, beginning after the 10 o'clock news.

Around the clock? Yup. We all thought it was a terrible investment of time. What was Bob thinking?

As it turns out, he was certainly ahead of his time. Had the ground blizzards occurred, there would have been a ton of on-air material archived to use for a brilliant promotion. But what if the blizzard condition never materialized? We would soon find out.

My "shift" began at 1:00 a.m. as Dave Towne went home to start his weekend. Up to that point, while it was windy and cold, no blizzard conditions had set up anywhere.

The half-hour cut-ins continued as we remained on-air (in 1982, most local stations still signed off from 1 a.m. to 6 a.m., using that window for station maintenance). By 3:30 a.m., it was clear to me that ground blizzards would not set up, but we faithfully executed every cut-in to keep whatever viewers still existed informed. By 5:00m a.m., we were getting rather punchy for lack of sleep. I still remember breaking out in hysterical laughter with fellow KGAN'er Tom Empy in between cut-ins.

Bob's call came in at 6:00 a.m. He told us to abandon our cut-ins and to go home and get some sleep, which we all gratefully did.

It was a risky decision, but had ground blizzards developed, Bob would have been recognized as a genius to remain on air, let alone having a ton of material for a powerful weather promotion. But it was a giant dud.

Bob was way ahead of his time. Now, with a decade or two of 24-hour broadcast days and non-stop cable news and weather under our belts, continuous coverage for severe weather of all types is no longer an extravagant pipe dream, but expected by the television audience. Job security? Sure. But there are times when we wonder if it's still worth it with media continuing to evolve. How this all sugars-out in the next few decades will be interesting. Time to let the young folks take the lead!

Tuesday, January 9, 2024
9:59 AM, Rainy, Windy, 34°F (Trace Of Slop)
Mile Marker 134

In a casual conversation with news director Andy
Fishman about how May will progress, I'll likely be
shifted over to spend a morning with the morning
crew. Makes perfect sense given I spent the first
two decades of my FOX 8 career on weekday
mornings. Not spending a little of my time with my
longtime partners like anchors Wayne Dawson and
Stefani Schaefer would seem odd. The body clock
shift may be a small challenge, but it's the last one
of that nature and worth the effort.

Wednesday, January 10, 2024
9:41 AM, Snow, 32°F (Powdered Doughnut Coating)
Mile Marker 133

Barometers settled to under 29.00" for a while last
evening between 6 PM and 10 PM. Our lowest here
in Novelty was 28.95" around 7:30 PM. Winds were
strong here, but much stronger in Buffalo. In a text
exchange with longtime friend Mike Cejka, he said
that Buffalo Airport hit 70 m.p.h., Dunkirk 74
m.p.h., and Watertown 78 m.p.h.! Another very
windy system heading in this weekend. Here we go.

While it may seem like it does periodically, the
atmosphere never takes a day off. It's always in
motion, always changing. It doesn't take Christmas
and New Year's Day off. It won't take weekends off.

Some of the most memorable storm systems that come to mind slammed us on a holiday or on a weekend. The atmosphere pays no attention to the calendar or clock. It's an aspect of meteorology I made peace with long ago, even as a young teenager, when I was grateful to see our local television meteorologists in Boston and Providence walking us through wild weather events in the 1970s. In my mind's eye, I can still see Art Lake, Barry Burbank, Bob Copeland, Dr. Fred Ward (original author of the word, "snizzle") and even prime-time meteorologists like Bruce Schwoegler, Don Kent, John Ghiorse, and Harvey Leonard spending long hours and days when a wild storm was the only thing in which anyone was interested. Each meteorologist was also there because they wanted to be there!

Big storms that didn't pay attention to the calendar or clock had a way of filtering out the narcissists who simply liked the thought of being on television. Big storm or not, when the weekend or holiday arrived, they did not want to be "hard at work." I've met and even worked with my fair share of them. As challenging as it made life in the weather office, the demands of the career eventually popped the illusion of egocentric colleagues to either make an adjustment or find another career.

That being said, let me make this absolutely clear! I consider myself amazingly blessed to have THE BEST meteorology colleagues with whom I have EVER had the chance of working! I shared this with both news director Andy Fishman and general manager Paul Perozini: As I approach retirement, I can honestly say that I will be reaching my television career finish line having the best workmates that I have ever had! Scott Sabol, Jenn Harcher, Alexis Walters, Dontaé Jones, and Mackenzie Bart are not only amazing colleagues, but cherished friends.

Whenever I entertained a young high school student for a tour of the weather office, I knew in a matter of minutes if their interest in what I did was driven by a pure passion for meteorology or because what I did simply looked glamorous. Even when I emphasized the 24/7/365 aspect of weather, those fueled by that pure passion for meteorology became excited at the thought of giving up a weekend or holiday to help the audience track a big weather event.

After almost five decades of helping the people around me navigate weather events, big and small, there is an interesting appeal to experience them on my backyard deck instead of on a weather set surrounded by radar displays and computer data. Yet, will I miss the adrenalin rush of helping a local television audience through a big weather event? I'm sure I will. It's what God infused into my spirit even before my first day of kindergarten! But He also gave me the joy of watching weather events unfold from the top of a backyard tree, a front porch, or from the cozy confines of a picture window.

I won't be giving up media altogether. I started my media career at age 15 on my hometown radio station, 1420-WBSM, New Bedford, Massachusetts.

I'll bookend my career by joining WKJA-FM (91.9), Heartfelt Radio in Barberton, Ohio, and on my web site, AndreBernier.com, and on my podcast WeatherJazz®.

Friday, January 12, 2024
11:46 AM, Thickening Clouds, 37°F (Bare Ground)
Mile Marker 131

God is amazing and so kind-hearted and patient.

On Thursday, I was forever searching for my key card that opened up the back door and the gate at work. I could not find it anywhere. I had to ask the security guard to open up the gate and the back door as I came in. I searched everywhere in the weather office. No sign of my key card. In a quiet moment, I then asked the Lord where my key card was... because He obviously knew where it was.

As I quieted my spirit and listened, the Holy Spirit gave me a vision of my left pants pocket of the suit I was wearing on Wednesday. But I passed my hand over the pockets earlier and felt nothing. Even so, the vision persisted and as I agreed to search there again when I returned home, an inexplicable peace washed over me. I knew I would find it there.

When I returned home last night, I pulled out the suit I wore on Wednesday. This time I pushed my hand INTO the left pocket. There it was. Key card found.

God is so good to help us in even the little things in life. In fact, the little things amaze me more than the big things.

Monday, January 15, 2024
10:40 AM, Anemic Sunshine, 8° (AM Low 0°F)
Mile Marker 128

The Holy Spirit tugged on me to make the effort to attend Faith Family Church's special Sunday night series conducted by Pastor Barb Camaneti called, "Two-Minute Warning." My legs were extraordinarily uncomfortable during the 90-minute period. I recognized it as a distraction from the enemy since it was a message from the Lord that I needed to not only hear, but to put in to action. Why am I wasting time chasing temporary endorphin rushes? In the end, they are empty. I want to please God, not exasperate Him!

Romans 8:22 (NLT) says, "For we know that all creation has been groaning as in the pains of childbirth right up to the present time." This passage came to mind as I watched the fifth volcanic eruption in the Reykjanes Peninsula (Iceland) bubble up early Sunday morning. This time, the lava moved into Grindavik, setting off several house fires. The lava covered Route 43, severing the electric and hot water lines to the city. More cracks have split open in the city. It has become uninhabitable. My heart sinks for the 4,000 displaced residents.

Even our intense cold (resulting in 1-2 feet of lake effect snow near Buffalo) is evidence of Earth's groaning. Sure, it may give broadcast meteorologists something to talk about, but it was never supposed to be this way. Sin ruined God's peaceful order. I wonder if broadcast meteorologists would have ever been needed if sin and rebellion had not entered the world? Would we still have been called to meteorology somehow? While I don't know the answer to questions like this, I am grateful that He instilled my passion for meteorology along with my desire to help people through the atmospheric groaning on this side of eternity.

I've had enough of the effects of sin (and that includes MY contribution to it). I need to operate in a way that points ahead to the joyful perfection that IS coming. ("But if we look forward to something we don't yet have, we must wait patiently and confidently." Romans 8:25 NLT).

Thursday, January 18, 2024
12:02 PM, Light Snow, 21°F (1" New Snow)
Mile Marker 125

Over my lifetime, I've thoroughly enjoyed learning new things, particularly about the atmosphere. When I was in elementary school through high school, the atmosphere itself was a great teacher along with many of my television meteorology mentors. Access to the meteorologists were limited to occasional letter exchanges, but the atmosphere was always there, ready to be observed and studied. There was no such thing as a boring weather day. Even when the atmosphere was "quiet," observing and analyzing the breeze, wind direction, temperature, dew point, and barometric pressure always held elements of fascination.

I had a favorite book on weather whose photos and articles I poured over hundreds of times hoping to glean a little more knowledge.

My NOAA weather radio "cube" purchased from Radio Shack provided hours and hours of entertainment, yes, far more than my favorite episodes of Gillian's Island or The Brady Bunch (more on that later). As delightful as these meteorological mentors were, not one of them could ever compare to the thrill of sitting under the tutelage of my Lyndon State College professor, Dr. Joe D'Aleo. He is as much of a weather nerd as all of his students (myself included), making the task of digging deep into what makes the atmosphere work so much fun. Even as the day of hanging up my television isobars approaches, I'm still using so much of what I learned from Dr. D'Aleo not only from my college years, but when he was my boss at The Weather Channel, and nowadays as I pour over his analysis and articles on WeatherBell.com.

Imagine my thrill of having him on my long-running podcast WeatherJazz® yesterday. Dr. D'Aleo was not just a "talking head" via Zoom, but came with charts and graphs galore. I felt like I was sitting in Climatology 101 all over again, learning even more.

Dr. D'Aleo has a web site dedicated to the study of climate from a realist's perspective. It's called IceCap.us. In his bibliography, I spotted something that made me smile. I was listed as a co-author of a peer-reviewed paper that was published by the National Weather Digest in 1982! Having MY name displayed right next to Dr. D'Aleo's in an official and academic capacity may have prompted an increase my hat size by two or three notches. I remember when he asked me to be his assistant in helping him pull together everything he needed for this paper on explosively developing east coastal storms (something we all call "bombogenesis").

Joe D'Aleo's continuing academic contribution is a real gift to meteorology. My guess is his works will be studied for decades in the same fashion that meteorology students today still study and find great value in the works Carl-Gustav Rossby (of the famed Rossby Wave Equation still in use today).

My name next to Dr. Joe D'Aleo's on a peer-reviewed paper from 1982? Hello. My name is André Bernier. My hat size is eleven.

Monday, January 22, 2024
8:02 AM, Filtered Sun, 16°F (5" Remain OG)
Mile Marker 121

Pastor Barb's special Sunday night study at Faith Family Church called, "2 Minute Warning," has been deep, revolutionary, and revelatory for me. There are aspects of my earthly journey on which I gave up long ago, yet God, in His mercy, lovingly encouraged me to address. Yes, He DID provide the victory! The two-minute warning has arrived. God has already designed a pathway to victory with my faith "football" in tact. Now it's not the time to give up!

Noah drove us to church and back last night. On the way home, I spotted one of several Waffle House restaurants just north of the church. Their iconic stand-alone building always makes me smile. I often think of the first time I ever visited them when I first moved to Marietta (Atlanta), Georgia in the spring of 1982 for the startup years of The Weather Channel.

Because our family members were early risers by default (my parents owned and operated a diner in New Bedford, Massachusetts), a big breakfast was always the norm. Finding a good breakfast hangout was a priority after moving to a totally unfamiliar city. There was a Waffle House not far from the original location of The Weather Channel off of Mt. Wilkinson Parkway located on Cobb Parkway. Like most Waffle Houses, it was quaint and inviting. It quickly became my go-to for the kind of breakfast that my parents insisted on at home. It was definitely comfort food.

During my first few weeks in Georgia, I vividly remember finding a seat in the middle of the counter once morning. I ordered breakfast and here it came with grits. I had never seen grits in my life! To me, they looked just like a small bowl of Cream Of Wheat, so I put a little butter in them. As the butter melted, I reached for the sugar dispenser. This got the attention of a rather gruff-looking character seated to my left. His eyebrows went up in disbelief as I poured sugar on my grits.

He looked at me with measured disgust and said something that will forever ring in my ears: "You must be a YANKEE!!!"

I quickly discerned that he meant no malice, but exclaimed his observation in a way that let me know that I would eventually draw a negative reaction. He offered a lesson in southern culture.

"Those are grits. Butter on them is good. Salt and pepper is good, too. But you may want to never let anyone see you put sugar on grits if you want to blend in to Georgia culture."

Until this encounter, I had no idea what grits were or what to do with them. I was genuinely grateful for his guidance and tried them with butter, salt, and pepper, and I liked them. Despite his gruff advice, I sensed his satisfaction with helping this northerner ease into life in the deep south.

I became such a regular at this Waffle House, that the pre-sunrise crew began to recognize my car and had my usual breakfast cooking on the grill before I ever got out of the car. It was not unusual to sit the counter and to have my breakfast being delivered without saying a single word! On the rare occasion I wanted something different, I tried my best to pull in and park away from the front window so that an order wasn't wasted.

I brought my parents to this Waffle House for breakfast when they came to visit me in Atlanta. They really enjoyed its similarity to The Diner Deluxe, the diner they owned and operated. One of the photos that has survived over the decades is the one I snapped in 1983.

Since there are few Waffle Houses in northern Ohio, visiting Waffle Houses in Lynchburg, Virginia during Noah's college years at Liberty University was something to which I always anticipated. Anytime I'm driving south on I-77 in the morning, I'll enjoy a big breakfast there. It's comfort food at its best!

Thursday, January 25, 2024
10:09 AM, Dense Fog, 47°F (No Snow Remains)
Mille Marker 118

I just received a book in the mail yesterday from my cherished longtime friend, Victoria, in northeast Vermont. It's a copy of Marty Engstrom's autobiography, <u>Marty On The Mountain</u>. Marty recently went home to be with the Lord on January 4th after a rich earthly journey of almost 87 years. He was one of the engineers that kept WMTW-8's transmitter running for decades, but what he is most remembered for is his down home, 30-second mountain weather briefing during the evening weather segments. His thick Maine accent and signature smile at the end of every weather briefing made him quite famous.

When I was in my early high school years, my sister lived in Essex Junction, Vermont. When we visited, she was excited to have me watch Marty's Mount Washington weather briefing. After sampling Marty for the first time, I could see why. Marty's window as a television engineer spanned from 1964 to 2002. Unfortunately, my only window for catching his segments was roughly 1973-1975 when my sister lived in Vermont, and again in my Vermont college years between 1977-1981. Despite my limited window to watch, you can easily call me a "<u>Marty On The Mountain</u>" fan. He is a cherished part of New England history. I'm looking forward to reading more about his time on the mountain.

Anytime I was able to watch his segments, I thought he had one of the coolest jobs "evah!"

Monday, February 5, 2024
7:29 AM, Clear, Fog, Frosty, 25°F (Bare Ground)
Mile Marker 107

The "End Of The Winter Outlook" aired on Friday at the end of the 6 PM newscast and went off without a hitch. As of now, I only have one more seasonal outlook to oversee. The summer outlook will air at the beginning of the May ratings book, a period that will prove interesting. In Bill Martin style, the station is already busy arranging clips of all kinds to showcase my forty-three year commercial television career.

It finally hit me this past weekend: I'll soon no longer need to drive fifty-two round-trip miles every weekday. The plus? No more driving through raging snowstorms, icy roads, severe thunderstorms, or waiting in stopped highway traffic for occasional accidents or construction. I won't miss the daily grind of compulsory weather content for the web, social media, and even on-air. What will I miss? The creative side of crafting interesting science and weather tidbits and the daily camaraderie with people with a common gift for media. It's the biggest paradigm shift since the move from the college class to the working class in the summer of 1981. That one didn't really sink in until just after Labor Day that year since my then girlfriend Sally (and other underclass men and women) returned to the campus while I did not. That was 43 years ago, a small eternity!

Thursday, February 8, 2024
7:51 AM, High Overcast, 38°F (Bare Ground)
Mile Marker 104

My weather tease from the FOX 8 Front Yard weather set on Wednesday looked more like one from April or May (without the greenery). Standing outside with nothing more than my suit jacket feel nice in a quirky way. At this time of year, despite the uncharacteristically warm breeze, there were no other life forms moving. No furry critters. No insects. No creepy crawlies. I suppose life in the outdoor weather center would have been boring if that was the case all the time.

This brings to mind many instances when I was not alone in the FOX 8 Front Yard. I've had everything from wandering cats to coyotes to skunks and possums wanting a little air time. I've had birds dive-bombing me if they thought I was getting too close to a nest they built in the bushes or a nearby tree. Then there was a curious bumblebee that flew up my pant leg during a noon weather segment. As I attempted to evacuate the bee out of my pant leg, it stung me while on live television! Thank goodness I am not allergic to bee stings.

Over the decades, I became less and less tolerant of the twice-yearly invasion of muckleheads (midges) in the Front Yard. In recent years, I gave up. Going outside during raging snowstorms, hailstorms, torrential rains, or amazingly high winds gave me a kind of adrenalin rush. As I always liked to say, I'll never get "current conditions" wrong since I'm standing IN it! But I waved the white flag when thousands upon thousands of muckleheads pasted themselves to the outside wall. All I had to do was open the glass doors in front to send thousands of them airborne, looking for my open mouth, ears, and nostrils. Who can speak while an innumerable swarm of muckleheads is looking for a way to interrupt a weather segment? No thanks!

Saturday, February 10, 2024
7:51 AM, Overcast, Warm, 50°F (Bare Ground)
Mile Marker 102

In the decades of executing weather segments from the outdoor weather set, there are some memorable (and in some cases, extreme and record-setting) weather events that unfolded on live television.

While the very first one occurred on a Saturday in June of 1988, my first summer in Cleveland, I was not on-air but at the annual WJW picnic at Hinkley Reservation. It was quite hot, but not too terribly humid (one of the only ways that clears the path for ambient air temperatures to exceed 100°F, something that is somewhat rare in Cleveland). Dick Goddard brought along his NOAA Weather Radio to keep track of the afternoon high since setting a new daily record was possible.

Just past four o'clock in the afternoon, I tuned in to see if we had set a record. The National Weather Service had just announced that Hopkins Airport reached 104°F, not only a new record for June 25th, but an all-time record high temperature.

I yelled over to Dick (who was playing softball), "Hey Dick! 104°F!"

He thought I was pulling his leg. I yelled over again, " Hey Dick. 104°F!"

He shook his head and muttered, "Nawwwwww."

I tried again a third time, "Hey Dick, 104°F!"

After a third time, he looked up at me and said, "Really?"

Never in recorded history died Cleveland ever experience a high of 104°F with dew points in the 50s°F

What are the chances that Cleveland experiences an all-time record on BOTH sides of the scale inside a 6 year span? Pretty slim, but it did happen, this time during "Newscenter 8 This Morning," on Wednesday, January 19, 1994. As was my custom for years, I was doing my morning weather segments from the "Front Yard" weather set. As we hit an ambient air temperature of -20°F, I was bringing all kinds of things outside to see how long it would take to freeze. A cup of water, an orange, a banana, and anything else we could think of became a curious side show. The banana became so hard, that I was able to use it to drive a nail into a board. The orange become so rock solid, that I was able to bounce it off the pavement like a "Superball" (until it broke in two)! The cup of water froze solid in forty minutes.

My noon weather segment that day was also live outside (that weather segment is available on Rumble). The snow was so cold and dry that I tried throwing the snow onto  the chromakey board. It never stuck, but slid right off the board.

Not only did I experience the two temperature extremes, but another (usually camera-shy) phenomenon: waterspouts! After many noon weather segments in the Front Yard where the potential for seeing waterspouts was high but never seen, the adrenalin flowed freely as not one, but THREE waterspouts came in to view behind me during one of my autumn weather segments. Being a distant cousin to the more powerful tornado, they looked like three small tornadoes in their initial stage.

While our outdoor weather set was protected by the FOX 8 building itself, high wind was sometimes a challenge for our heavy chromakey board on wheels

if the wind direction was just right. I quickly
learned to abandon the chromakey segments if I
expected gusts to exceed twenty miles-per-hour
from the northwest or north. This avoided the
"green screen" from blowing over during a live
segment. But every once in a while I either
underestimated the wind speeds or misjudged the
wind direction. The result made for memorable
television as my "weather graphics board," despite
some very heavy counterweights, blew over. Over
the years, this probably happened at least a half-
dozen times.

Tuesday, February 13, 2024
6:37 PM, Cloudy, 31°F (Bare Ground)
Mile Marker 99

While my WeatherJazz® audience has known about
my plans to retire on May 22nd since late last year,
I brought everyone else up to speed via Instagram
and Facebook using the "Mile Marker 99" as a
vehicle today. I am truly honored and humbled by
so many well-wishers including NBC's Kelly
O'Donnell with whom I worked when she anchored
Newscenter 8 This Morning (in our CBS affiliate
days).

There are days when approaching this new chapter
seems surreal. It's all beginning to sink in deeper
with every passing day. There's a sense of peace
and joy now, but I have a sense that peace will
dominate this final leg once I finish ironing out all of
the confusing government rules and regulations

that go along with planning for a new season. Can they make it any harder? (I hope they don't see that as a challenge for future generations.)

Wednesday, February 14, 2024
10:12 AM, Clearing Skies, 30°F (Bare Ground)
Mile Marker 98

I was never officially an "intern" per se, but I had something far better when I was in high school. That was my three year "apprenticeship" at 1420-WBSM in New Bedford. What I learned there was invaluable. The on-air grooming I received got me ready for what was to come.

Just before my senior college year, I had the chance to feed twelve New England radio stations every other weekend morning thanks to a recommendation from college classmate Brian Durst to then WPRI-TV-12 meteorologist Tom Chisolm who was starting a new weather service to radio stations. The best part was that it was my first paid weather position. Again, it was not an internship, but something better.

While I was not in a position to offer an internship in Iowa, Georgia, or Minnesota, I finally had the chance to take on summer interns in Cleveland. It was an opportunity to help equip the next generation of meteorologists while giving students the chance to participate in the daily grind of putting together weather segments.

In the summers that I opened up an internship opportunity, I prayerfully considered every cover letter and resumé that arrived. While I can't speak for others who make that decision, I can tell you what I was looking for. It wasn't experience. It's wasn't knowledge. (I still remember getting cover letters from students who told me what they were going to teach ME, a big turn off!). No, I was looking for someone who was humble and teachable. One of my favorite letters over the decades came from an Ohio State University student by the name of Brian Westfall. His hopes to be able to learn as much as possible in the summer ahead was framed with a sweet humility. God's Holy Spirit confirmed that this was the candidate I was waiting for. (By contrast, it was the same year I received the boastful letter mentioned above.)

Brian now works as a contractor for NOAA at the Akron-Canton Airport and loves his work. He waited a long time for his chance to break into the weather business, but his steadfast determination eventually got him there. This was exactly the kind of person that I wanted to equip and encourage.

Like my longtime colleague at KMBC-TV in Kansas City, Bryan Busby, my joy bubbles over when I take a collective look at where all of my interns ended up. Most of them are enjoying a satisfying career in meteorology in some way. After graduating with his degree in meteorology, one of them even worked his way through the media ranks and ended up taking my spot on weekday mornings when I moved to weekday evenings in 2007. That's right.

Meteorologist Scott Sabol was once my summer intern during his college years in St. Louis.

Other former interns have enjoyed career stops in television markets in Rochester, NY; Syracuse, NY; Bluefield, WV; Charleston, WV; Wilkes-Barre Scranton, PA; Erie, PA; Columbus, OH; Plattsburgh, NY; Fargo, ND; and Fort Myers, FL.

I would be remiss if I didn't make one honorable mention here. Lauren Hilko Morton was arguably my best intern. Not only was every task I sent before her executed with both speed and excellence, but she actually anticipated what I would need and do it without my asking. It was her keen ability to intentionally watch everything being done to try to anticipate what would be helpful. Lauren spent three years at a television station in Fargo, North Dakota after her graduation, then returned home to Ohio expanding on her meteorology degree by getting her airline dispatcher license. Before recently entering her most important role as a full-time Mom, Lauren accepted a managerial role with one of the major airlines. Seeing her success makes me proud, but better yet was when Sally and I were invited into her inner world at her wedding some years ago. Her life team up with Robert was a brilliant move. As a family, Robert and Lauren bring me confident hope in the next few generations.

Over the decades, my one request from any intern I took under my wing was this: When you get settled into your careers and if you are able, pass it on... that is, pour into the next generation behind you.

In this way, my career propagates like a wave where a pebble is initially dropped in a pond well beyond my last day at WJW-TV.

Monday, February 19, 2024
10:09 AM, A NACITS Sky, 33°F (1" On Ground)
Mile Maker 93

Aside from my focus on a few of the unique and even interesting challenges that shaped my career as a television meteorologist, one may think that it was (by in large) all rainbows and roses. But the very fact that I'm talking about rainbows points to the fact that you need a heavy rain shaft (often a violent thunderstorm) moving away from you (and the sun behind you) in order to see a rainbow. Storms in life are in inevitable. There were plenty in my over four decades of television. As difficult as it may have been at times, I have always relied on the raw passion for my craft to help me navigate those days, weeks, months, and even years. This is true no matter what God designed for any one of us.

Had God not instilled the gifts He gave me, I likely would have abandoned this path long ago.

I won't spend a lot of time on this part of this painting, but the last thing I want to do is to completely mask it with rainbows and roses.

Before my lengthy thirty-six plus year tenure in Cleveland, Sally and I spent almost three years in

Minneapolis. You can read more about the specifics and the people who made that part of life's journey special in my book, The Extra Mile (available on Amazon). It was at the NBC affiliate, KARE-11, that I was exposed to one of the most unique weather sets in all of television. It was an outdoor weather set with a greenhouse type access to the news studio. When we moved to Cleveland, I brought the idea with me since no one in Cleveland was doing weather segments in this way. Building the outdoor set was done in several stages. I covered a few aspects of this journey earlier.

At one point, not long after our affiliate switch from CBS to FOX in 1994, we had a management change. We suddenly had a general manager who had the strong opinion that an outdoor weather set was absurd. The large and beautiful cedar deck that our previous and beloved GM had constructed for the outdoor weather segments was, without any announcement, totally removed in one weekend. When I left the station to start my weekend on a Friday, we had a stunning, specially designed outdoor weather set thanks to general manager Virgil Dominic. When I returned on Monday, thanks to then general manager Bob Rowe, it was totally gone, replaced by lawn. The outdoor weather segments that took so much work and effort to create were canceled. All of my segments were brought back into the studio. I was devastated and deflated. But I hung in there hoping that someday those unique weather segments would return.

They did.

Just as suddenly as the weather deck was gone, after a short season (maybe a year or two), FOX brass from HQ (we were then owned by FOX) stopped in one day to announce that Bob Rowe was no longer our general manager.

The very next day, I walked into then chief engineer Mark Thomas' office. The big news was what happened the day before. Then I asked him if he would have one of the engineers set me up for a noon outdoor weather segment. It didn't take long for Mark's smile to let me know that we had weathered a challenging season, but that all changed in several hours. All of the equipment to make outdoor weather segments happen was put in storage, waiting for this day.

Not only was it set up for that day's "Front Yard" weather segment, but Mark told engineer Jim Snell to install it in a way that was permanent, something which may have never happened without that challenging year or two.

With my PSC (personal services contract) about to expire, I insisted on the inclusion of a clause that allowed me the option of dissolving the contract if station managers ever took away the outdoor weather segments, again something on which I would have never insisted before that difficult period. Would I have ever exercised it? Probably not, but I wanted the option available.

By the next contract cycle, the outdoor weather segments had become such a signature staple of

FOX 8, that I was comfortable without the outdoor weather clause. Since then, the outdoor space has been landscaped and upgraded several times to take full advantage of showcasing the sometimes wild Lake Erie lakeshore weather. It truly makes for great television.

A few other equally "dark" and challenging periods come to mind, but there is no need to elaborate here. My point in sharing the above story is to serve as an encouragement. If God has called and equipped you to do something, He will also equip you with what you need to not only survive those dark seasons, but to someday make sweet lemonade out of the lemons you may be required to hold in your lap for a season.

Know that a rainbow awaits you on the other side of any severe thunderstorm.

Wednesday, February 21, 2024
11:00 AM, Filtered Sun, 49°F (Shady CC Remain)
Mile Marker 91

My exposure to television production during my early high school years (my freshman and sophomore years at the then brand new New Bedford High School, 1973-1975) added fuel to my desire to learn as much as I could by hanging out at any media outlet that would allow me to.

The brand new New Bedford High School opened its doors in September of 1973 when I was a freshman.

It was a stunning, state-of-the-art campus. There were two places I loved the hang out. The first spot was more transitory in nature. There was a weather station display on the second floor "core," a circular corridor that connected four arms of classrooms (identified by color: green, gold, tan, and blue... with most of my classes as well as my "homeroom" mainly in the "green house.") It was connected to an instrument cluster on the high school's roof. I made a point swinging by there as often as possible to see what the wind and temperature were doing. It was similar, but bigger than the weather station at Normandin Junior High School. That one was in a science classroom whose teacher let me monitor the unit while I was perched on stool so I could watch it until it was time for classes to start.

The second (and probably more important) place where I spent my spare time was in the high school's television studio and lab. The teacher who presided over the studio was Barry Manghan. He soon realized that he simply could not get rid of me, so he put me to work in the distribution area. I was responsible for loading taped programs and sending them through a patch board to classrooms that would watch them for a part of their coursework. It was where I also learned how to operate a video switcher and how to maintain the (then) black and white cameras. Eventually, when it came time to produce a student-led lunchtime newscast that would "air" in all four dining commons at lunchtime, Barry figured out a way to have me do weather segments.

I remember one such newscast well... it was just before the Christmas break. Barry insisted I dress up as Santa and give a Christmas forecast as if I was at the North Pole. I wasn't going to argue if it meant "on-air" time. Santa it was, pillow in my belly and all!

A few decades ago after internet email became established, I received a surprise email from Barry, who at that time was retired and living in Florida. He did a search and was delighted to find me doing something I was bent on doing as a high school student and took the time to say hello. I was humbled that he remembered me as we recalled the days when he simply could not get rid of me in a place I loved hanging out.

Saturday, February 24, 2024
7:26 AM, Cloudy, 21°F (Frozen, Bare Ground)
Mile Marker 88

Some stories are worth duplicating if it brings something to the new "painting." I wrote about Channel 6 (New Bedford) meteorologist Charlie (Chuck) Taylor in my book, The Extra Mile, but have yet to spend time adding that part off my life to this work. I would be remiss if I did not use a few brush strokes to fill that into the big picture because it was significant in my early years growing up.

When I was in my early teens, the ABC affiliate (then WNEV-TV-6) had its studios on County Street

in New Bedford. Charlie Taylor was the chief
meteorologist at the time. Somehow, Charlie
allowed me to come in to shadow him as he went
through his routine. As I remember, I biked there
3.8 miles from our Sutton Street home. Charlie
could not have been any nicer. He explained
everything he did. I drank it all in. Somehow, I
kept returning. I started doing some of his menial
tasks for him whenever I could. I truly wanted him
to see me as helpful.

My persistence in showing up eventually led to my
being "adopted" by the news staff, so much so that
the receptionist no longer required me to "sign in"
before heading up to the second floor newsroom.

I parked and locked my bike on the inside of a
cement lattice that faced the big picture window of
the art director's office. While his name escapes
me, I can still "see" his face in my mind's eye. He
once pulled me aside to let me know that a group of
boys once made their way inside the cement lattice,
examining my bike trying to figure out a way to
steal it. Seeing this, he quickly ran up to his
window and knocked on it, shaking his finger.
Busted! They ran off when they saw that someone
saw them. He wanted me to know so that I made
sure my bike chain was secure every time I visited,
and that he would make sure to keep an eye on
things whenever I was there.

With time, I became a part of the fabric of WNEV-6
and was given access to every part of the building
without question. This proved very helpful to
Charlie one day. Apparently stuck in traffic, he was

delayed in getting to the station. Knowing his routine intimately, I simply started doing all of the work that he would do so that he would not be rushed when he arrived. He was so late, I wondered if he would even make it for the start of the newscast at 6 p.m.

I even put together a forecast, made my way to the studio, and assembled that forecast on the magnetic board that held whitish magnetic letters against a chromakey blue background. This is how the forecast was displayed back then.

Charlie finally arrived, visibly irritated by whatever it was that delayed him. His countenance totally changed when he saw that everything was done. He was shocked that the forecast was done and set up on the magnetic board, too. He checked my work. Aside from a minor forecast temperature tweak, he let all of my work stand.

I biked back home in time to watch Charlie's weather segment at 6:15 p.m. and told everyone that everything they are about to see from the weather maps to the forecast "pages" was 100% my work! My heart was beating fast with adrenalin as I watched Charlie Taylor display my work on television.

After a few years, Charlie left WNEV-6 and landed in Louisville, Kentucky where he enjoyed a solid twenty-year career that was cut short by colon cancer. He passed away at age 53 in 1997. Judging from all of the newspaper articles written, "Chuck" was well loved and respected at WHAS-11. I learned about his death from the AMS Bulletin some time later and I was heartbroken. I remember dedicating an entire morning show weather production to his memory hoping that he would see it from a heavenly portal. I briefly exchanged emails with Charlie's son, letting him know how much his father shaped my own career. I am hopeful that someday, we will meet again in heaven, where I can thank him once more for being so patient and kind to a twelve-to-thirteen year old weather nerd.

Thursday, Leap Day, February 29, 2024
4:40 PM, NACITS, 33°F (1" At Sunrise, CC Now)
Mile Marker 83

Perspective. Paradigm shift. I was watching the noon weather segment from the NBC affiliate in Twin Falls, Idaho in my studio today. The meteorologist looked SO young! Then I had to stop myself. I was doing the exact same thing when I lived in Cedar Rapids, Iowa when I was just barely over 22 years old! In fact, when I moved from Minneapolis to Cleveland and started at WJW-TV, I was 28 years old! Where did all that time go? As my mother once said not long before leaving this world at age 88, "Don't blink!" It's my intention to live every day in the next twenty years with focus and eternal purpose. Doing so without the Lord Jesus would be a grave error. Thank God I don't have to do it alone.

Friday, March 1, 2024
9:39 AM, NACITS, 36°F
Mile Marker 82

We often hear the term, "the good old days." Why can virtually everyone relate? Is it that those days were really that much better, or is it something else? With over six decades of observation under my belt, I've come to the conclusion that it's something else.

Every generation that ever lived and will come into the picture in the future has and will find that life becomes more and more complicated as we prepare for careers, families, and more. During our adolescent years, we yearn for those days ahead without realizing the complexities and the challenges that wait for us. To use an appropriate cliché, we are living out our carefree days. We aren't concerned about food and shelter. Our parents are the ones dutifully taking care of those. When we were in our elementary school years, this looked so easy because our parents made it look effortless, thus the "good old days." (Of course now we know this wasn't the case!)

That elbow room gave me the opportunity to focus on some of the amazing miracles that chased me down. Each one moved me closer to my destiny. Each one also confirmed that there was a heavenly Father who took deep interest in those things that were important to me, especially the small things. Part the Red Sea? No problem. Raise Jesus from the dead after three days? Piece of cake. But intensely interested in the smallest detail in one person's life? Why would He do so? Answer: Because we are His children.

While I already cover this story in my book, The Extra Mile, sometimes a good story needs repeating and revisiting. It may have happened over fifty years ago, but for me, the marvel has never diminished. Only God could have done this!

After Channel 6's Charlie Taylor introduced me to a weather data stream on the "long wave" band (just below the AM radio band) aimed to pilots called "TWEBs" (or Transcribed Weather Broadcasts) where hourly observations for more than a dozen New England airports were disseminated, I longed to buy a multi-band radio that included the "LW" band. The biggest hurdle for a fourteen-year-old is that a multi-band radio was well outside of my budget.

Somehow, I saw an article on how anyone, with a few inexpensive electronic parts from Radio Shack, could convert a standard transistor AM radio into a long wave receiver. The parts cost me no more than two dollars. Using tools in my father's workshop, I went through the meticulous work of soldering tiny capacitors, resistors, and diodes to small terminals in my opened radio-cassette recorder. I took my time. I wanted to do it right.

The time came to plug in the radio and to try out out. The long-wave station I was hoping to hear came from Boston Logan Airport on 382 kHz (the AM band stops at 530 kHz). After a few deep breaths, I plugged it in at my homework desk in the finished basement. All I heard was white noise and static. I turned the tuner slowly back and forth. More white noise and static. After a few minutes, it was clear that I was not going to hear what I had hoped. I was crushed.

All this happened during one of the colder months of the year since I was in our finished basement wearing a wool sweater. Something behind me must have caught my attention since I began to spin counter-clockwise on my desk seat. The radio-cassette recorder, open with its electronic boards exposed, was on the left side of my desk. In only one second, the wool sleeve on my sweater caught some of the electronic board's sharp, soldered connections. My radio-cassette recorder went flying off the desk. I watched in what seemed like slow-motion as the unit crashed to the tiled, cement floor. Pieces and parts snapped off and flew all over the floor. Not only was my meticulous work ruined, but it was likely that my prized unit was totally broken beyond repair. I could have cried.

After gathering all of the pieces and parts, not only did some of my soldered electronics snap off, but there were original parts that were dislodged from the circuit boards and I had absolutely no idea where to solder them back. My prized possession gifted to me for Christmas by my parents was likely headed for the garbage bin.

I wondered if I would get any sound from it now.

What did I have to lose? I could at least plug it in to see what would happen. Honestly, I thought perhaps I would see sparks and smell smoke. After cautiously securing the plug into a nearby outlet, I was relieved that nothing happened. Turning it on was probably going to net a different outcome. After a moment or two, I turned the radio on and turned the volume up. I heard something. Voices through a little white noise. Amazed, I turned it up:

"Transcribed weather broadcast, aviation forecast. Synopsis...."

I had a hard time wrapping my head around it! It was the National Weather Service long wave station from Boston Logan Airport at 382 kHz!!! Yet, on the desk right next to the unit were more than a dozen electronic pieces that flew off of my radio-cassette recorder. How could this be? I went from wanting to cry to wanting to leap for joy.

God knew that the ability to glean that weather data was important to me and that I would dial in 382 kHz daily for years, which I did. Over the decades, I still marvel at how God did that. Whether He sent one of His angels or whether it was Jesus Himself who calculated the force and angle needed to convert the AM band to the LW band points to a miraculous moment designed to bring joy to one of His adopted children. It goes well beyond coincidence. In fact, let me unequivocally declare that I am fully persuaded that there are no such things as coincidences. A new friend of mine from Connecticut recently sent me a book about these life encounters. The author calls them, "God Winks." Indeed, and amen.

Saturday, March 2, 2024
10:37 AM, Drizzle, 44°F
Mile Marker 81

When I first started doing weekend weather on my hometown radio station, WBSM (New Bedford, MA) at age 15, suddenly weekends took on a special dimension. Other than occasional material perks that came my way (like WBSM's annual employee Christmas dinner and use of station equipment and studio production time when they were not in use), I did not receive compensation for my contribution. I never asked for it nor did the thought ever cross my mind. I was given a rare gift of professional experience and I loved immersing myself in that atmosphere.

While most of my high school classmates were sleeping in or enjoying some down time from academia, I was up before sunrise to ride my bike from my boyhood home on Sutton Street near New Bedford Airport to Pope's Island just across the Fairhaven Bridge three miles away. The only time I remember not biking to the station was when it was snowing. I would call my forecasts in to news anchor Jim Phillips by phone. Without knowing, my legs became quite strong from the twice weekly bike ride back home from Pope's Island (which was all uphill).

Once I earned my driver's license at age 17, Mom would occasionally encourage me to drive the family car to the station to get experience driving. There wasn't much traffic at that hour on weekends, so it was a good time to refine my skills on the road.

At age 16, I did land a job at a local McDonald's and was able to stay off of the work schedule on weekend mornings to accommodate my forecast duties at WBSM. While it made for a long day at times, I always looked forward to my mornings at the station as the best part of my weekend.

Despite becoming a radio fixture on weekends in my hometown on a very popular 5,000 watt AM station, it was not enough. I looked for creative ways to refine my communication skills. During my junior and senior years in high school, I asked if I could swing by the office to provide a weather forecast to the student body during the morning announcements. My audience included over four thousand classmates during "homeroom time." I did this without fail from 1975 until I graduated in 1977.

At Lyndon State College in Lyndonville, Vermont (now University of Northern Vermont), my outlets included the LSC Weatherphone (a recorded forecast that local residents could call for updated forecasts), our on-campus television station, and our on-campus radio station, WWLR-FM. Without any of these outlets, preparing for a career in "real-world, network" television would have much more challenging.

Nowadays, anyone wanting to refine on-air skills have new tools available. New media (such as Rumble and podcasting platforms) takes media and puts it into the hands of virtually anyone. It will be interesting to see how this new media works into the potential audience routines over time. Like the Buggles once sang in their 1979 hit, "Video Killed The Radio Star," internet video outlets may cause traditional over-the-air stations to become irrelevant! Time will tell.

Friday, March 8, 2024
10:14 AM, Mostly Cloudy, Sunny Glints, 46°F
Mile Marker 75

The volume of weather data used to be very costly to obtain, not only from the National Weather Service, but from third party weather data vendors. Fortunately for anyone working in meteorology, the cost was passed on to our employers, but the data available to weather enthusiasts and armchair meteorologists was severely limited until the flow of data suddenly went from a trickle to that of one of Iceland's limitless, continuous waterfalls.

Yet, there is a sentimental attachment to the simplicity of watching clouds move and change, or listening to the current conditions feed from NOAA Weather Radio (with the main frequencies at 162.55 MHz and 162.40 MHz, well above the FM band). Once thought of as "high-tech" in the 1970s, this method of data collection and analysis is quite

Jurassic. Yet, by removing the glut of online weather and model data, something interesting happens. Our observational and reasoning skills become better refined. We are forced to intensely analyze the atmosphere through our eyes instead of watching webcams from the surface and sharp images from the latest GOES stationary satellites.

As a high school student in the 1970s, would I have liked perusing all of the data available to us today? You bet! On the same hand, I'm glad we didn't. It forced anyone with a passion for meteorology to examine and study the sky with their own eyes.

While I envy the youth of today for whom the Lord has gifted with a deep passion for weather, I also see evidence of an unhealthy reliance for all of the computer modeling data available. One of my revered college meteorology professors, Col. Merle Woodall, reminded all of us ad nauseam that the model data "was NOT gospel," but only "guidance." We always need to ask ourselves if the models are doing a good job or not. Does the computer "future simulation" make sense based on observation and historical recall? If not, how should the meteorological referee adjust?

Too often, I have witnessed my younger protégées react to every run of the model data with knee-jerk, hook line and sinker reactions instead of using the simulations critically.

One vivid example comes to mind.

It was a Friday morning in the 1990s. I walked in to the station at 3 a.m. and looked over the latest model data. Like the prior few days, it pointed to a major weekend Ohio Valley snowstorm. Winter Storm Watches and Warnings were posted for all of Ohio. The NWS forecast called for a 6-12" accumulation of snow.

I was excited until something caught my attention. The high pressure system in central Canada was over 31.00" and the air was cold and very dense north of Michigan. This raised my suspicion. My next step was to check 3-hour pressure tendencies in the Ohio Valley. Without exception, they were all trending upward, even closer to the developing surface low south of Memphis. All this pointed to a surface storm track that would be "pushed" much farther south than the models suggested.

Going against the grain, and with great caution, I explained to the audience what I saw. The forecast I put out for Saturday was for no more than flurries at best. Everyone else in Cleveland was declaring that we were in for quite a snowstorm.

By noon, Cleveland NWS had dropped all Winter Storm Watches and Warnings and essentially scaled back the threat of snow to minimal. They finally saw what I did.

So what happened weather wise?

Not only was there no significant snowfall in northern Ohio, but our sky was near cloudless! Bright sun with a deck off cirrus along the southern horizon along with intensely cold air. The farthest north the snow got was Charleston, West Virginia.

It was one of those satisfying moments in my career where all of the focus on critical thinking in my college classes taught by Col. Woodall and Dr. Joe D'Aleo paid off in a big way. In my humble opinion, that aspect of critical thinking isn't being taught like it should in colleges and universities whether it's in the atmospheric science, political science, or any other discipline. It is something I tried my best to impart in the last 495 days as I prepare to begin life outside of WJW-TV.

When I announced my plans to leave WJW-TV to my colleagues in the weather office last May, I asked them to make a switch. Instead of the term of endearment they liked using when I arrived every day, I asked them to use the word, "Coach." They all took it seriously and did so immediately. As I had hoped, they took my request literally and always listened closely whenever I thought we needed to consider adjustments in our forecast end product.

Tuesday, March 12, 2024
8:54 AM, NACITS, 47°F (Little Snow Remains)
Mile Marker 72

NACITS... N.A.C.I.T.S.

It's an acronym that has been a part of my DNA for over four decades. Virtually anyone (and perhaps thankfully almost everyone) in northeast Ohio is familiar with it: Not A Cloud In The Sky.

Just last night, a delightful brother in Christ at the station, Kevin, stopped me on his rounds in the newsroom and was happy to hear me call for "NACITS" last night. I took a few moments to tell him how NACITS got its start.

After college graduation, I was one of the fortunate group to have started in my chosen field immediately in Iowa. While it may have been more than a thousand miles away from New England, I could not have hand selected a better place or television station to begin to learn my craft.

I always liked to be unique and expressive. Being a bit of a writer, I enjoyed using words to paint an accurate verbal picture of what the audience would encounter.

One day, the sky was as clear as it could be on a summer day. I could have just as easily wrote "Clear and Warm" on the sheet that I would walk down to where my forecast was typed into an electronic font generator (back then known as "Chyron"). Instead, I wrote: "Not A Cloud In The Sky."

A few minutes later, the young lady who was setting my electronic type stopped by the weather office with my forecast sheet in her hand.

"It won't fit," she said referring to "Not A Cloud In The Sky."

I looked at may forecast sheet for a moment and wondered what to do. "Clear and warm," was too boring. Then I looked at the first letter in each word: N.... A.... C.... I.... T.... S. Hmmmm. NA-sits?

That didn't have a good sound. NA-kits? Yes! NA-kits, with a hard "C" sound!

On that summer day in 1981, NACITS (NA-kits) was born. NACITS was an instant hit in Iowa. To a lesser degree, I used it at The Weather Channel. Then on my first day on-air at KARE-11 in Minneapolis, I had the opportunity to use it. During the post-newscast morning meeting, VP of News Tom Kirby looked at his notes, then looked at me.

"NACITS," he asked?

Tom cocked his head, smirked, and then said, "LOVE it!"

NACITS followed me to Cleveland in 1988, an acronym I used liberally every time skies were totally clear.

A decade or so after I started my career at WJW-TV, I was watching The Weather Channel when a relatively new weather anchor was pointing to a large dry area. My ears perked up when he used the term, "NACITS!" Because I was still in touch with many people at TWC, I sent an email to the OCM (on-camera meteorologist) manager wondering how this new anchor got a hold of an acronym I invented. The answer came quickly. The new OCM I was watching grew up in Tuscarawas

County, Ohio, watching me through his younger years growing up. What an honor to be emulated!

Will anyone at FOX 8 use it after I hang up my television isobars? I can't answer that question beyond being humbled and grateful if someone else grabs it and runs with it.

Saturday, March 16, 2024
2:24 PM, Sunny, Breezy, 57°F
Mile Marker 68

Thursday (March 14) was a LONG day at FOX 8. Both Dontaé and I were surprised by the tornadic thunderstorms that erupted just inside our DMA, part of a large outbreak of tornadoes from Ohio to Texas along a cold front. I did not have to consider whether or not to stay past my usual 7 p.m. departure. With Mackenzie on her way to Europe for nine days, leaving Dontaé to potentially cover tornado coverage solo was not something I was about to do. It was only fifteen minutes later that the first tornado warning edged into the FOX 8 viewing area. Dontaé and I were off to the races, so-to-speak.

We spent two continuous hours tacking a large EF-2 tornado. While damage to the town of Plymouth was extensive, we were thankful that much of the ten-mile path was over farmland.

The evening went as well as it could have. There were no fatalities despite the damage. While I was completely exhausted, I drove home surrounded by bright flashes of lightning as the midnight hour approached. Will this be the last night of tornado coverage before May 22? Only God knows. But if it is, there is an element of satisfaction having "finished well." Remember, earlier in my career, I dreaded long stretches of continuous tornadic coverage. In fact, I hated it. My voice was often taxed to failure. The waves of adrenalin mimicked mini-panic attacks. Not this time, or anytime in the last handful of years.

What changed?

I dwelt on that as I was winding down at home. Sally had gone to bed and Noah had been asleep for hours. The house was as quiet as it could be. While I thanked the Lord for supplying me with what I needed to "finish well," He reminded me of two things. The first were my own prayers asking for help over the decades. The second were the prayers of my mother who was in heaven and finally understood my desire to grow past my anxiety at covering severe weather outbreaks. She saw me struggle when she was still walking on this side of eternity. I could see how she wanted to understand what I was going through, but couldn't quite wrap her head around something that I didn't fully grasp myself. I'm convinced that she was given perfect clarity in heaven, and that her prayers were specific and powerful. God was (and is) faithful. Patience has never been one of my shining virtues, but patience is what God needed me to exercise over the course of my career so that I could reach my television finish line having accomplished the course having "won my race" (1 Corinthians 9:24).

It would not have been too terribly satisfying to hang up my television isobars with unresolved issues. Doing so would have meant not finishing the race! Praise God, with 68 days remaining and the finish line coming into focus, I can now honestly smile in knowing that I will cross that boundary hearing the Lord's encouraging words, "well done!"

It didn't take too long for me to drift off into a happy, restorative, an dreamless sleep, the kind described in the book of Proverbs, Chapter 3.

Good Friday, March 29, 2024
8:24 AM, NACITS, Frosty, 27°F
Mile Marker 54

There's a measure of awe that increases with every day that passes by, especially as we approach a new border. For the last four hundred or so days, I could not put my finger on it. I can now do so. I recognize it as the feed reel on a reel-to-reel tape machine dizzily spinning faster and faster. It's a sensation I've not had to process since July of 1988.

This new border is not like the kind of state boundary change that happens while one is driving on a cross-country trip. Typically, those happen without much realization until you see one of those giant "welcome" signs that make you realize you are now in a different state. In most cases, the scenery hasn't changed much if at all. This approaching border is different. It's not so much the "terminus" of something as it is a gateway to a new beginning and new season.

I've been blessed by not having to cross many of these boundaries in my life and career. I believe that by reviewing each of the border crossings in my life journey thus far, it will help me navigate the one I cross in fifty-four days with positive finesse. Let's get started.

Initially, I never recognized the first two borders until now. Perhaps it was because I didn't have enough life perspective, but it's worth visiting briefly before moving on to all of them.

Border Crossing #1: September 3, 1977.

This was the day my family moved me from my Sutton Street home and moved me into my college dorm on the campus of what was then called Lyndon State College in Lyndonville, Vermont, as a college freshman. Rather than rewrite something that I've already processed, here is an excerpt from an email recalling (Labor Day, Monday, September 5, 1977) that I sent to my younger brother many years ago:

(My family) met me for breakfast at Saga (Stevens Dining Hall) and everyone seemed strangely perfectly at home sitting with me in the Stevens Dining Hall. It felt like putting on an old, comfortable shoe! Perhaps its was a shadow of the fun we would have together in the decades to come during family outings on Burke Mountain. The fog lifted while we had breakfast and the sun broke out gloriously. A cloudless, blue sky.

Breakfast itself was a big blur...but what wasn't was having to say so-long. You had parked in the Wheelock parking lot (the red brick dorm between the main dorm complex and the Student Center). It felt very strange... last minute instructions... about staying safe, eating well, studying hard, and Dad and Mom's expression of love (as of that time not verbal). Watching the maroon car pull away, down the hill and eventually out of sight was probably the oddest concoctions of emotions I had ever experienced, even to this day.

On one end of the spectrum, a great adventure had just begun! I was excited and joyous to be in a deep northern climate where deep drifts would soon surround me every morning.... surrounded by weather equipment galore and hopes and dreams of learning meteorology.... being in control... holy smokes!... being in control.

It was probably then that I realized that my steps were no longer guided, and dependent on Mom and Dad. I was in control... the first major change to one of independence. Then the mix of a "soft" kind of sadness... realizing that I was no longer a permanent resident of 78 Sutton. That for three more summers, I'd temporarily come home, and then likely head out into the world solo. I suddenly felt lonely... intensely lonely... and at the same time, thrilled and feeling like the greatest adventure of my life lay straight ahead.....

....And indeed it was.

Border Crossing #2: May 1981

While I no longer remember the specific day, I do remember this happened a week or so before my 22nd birthday on May 22. I was in Iowa by then. Sally graciously drove me from New Bedford (with a new suit that my parents bought me and my mother tailored to my size along with my modest belongings) to Cedar Rapids with a brief stop at Sally's home in Cleveland.

Beginning my television career at this major eastern Iowa powerhouse television station was unnerving. If one could cage all the butterflies that were generated during those first few summer months, you would have needed a cage that spanned the size of the entire Hawkeye state.

I must have been too busy to realize that I had crossed a life border, that is, until Labor Day 1981. After Labor Day, something seemed extraordinarily odd. Indeed there was. For the first time since 1964, I was not heading into a classroom to begin a school year. The only class in which I found myself in 1981 was the working class. Feeling like there was something missing was an understatement. It took a decade or more before that odd September feeling faded.

Border Crossing #3: February 26-27, 1982

This was the first "legitimate" shift from one career position to another. In only nine months, I had made many new friends and was able to make Iowa, a state over a thousand miles away from where I grew up, my new home base. It helped that one of my college classmates, Brian Durst, lived a few doors down from me in the apartment complex I called home. Brian was hired at KCRG-9, so we were competitors, but remained close friends.

While the management at KGAN-2 was very good to me, I kept my eye on the development stages of a new, national cable television network in Atlanta simply called The Weather Channel. My former professor of meteorology, Dr. Joe D'Aleo, co-founder of The Weather Channel, offered me a job at the new start up with a report date of March 1, 1982.

My last day at KGAN-2 was Friday, February 26, 1982. After doing the morning CBS network cut-ins and the local noon weather segment, and after a short celebration lunch with my co-workers, I was on the road. Cedar Rapids was in the rear view mirror. Adrenalin fueled my afternoon in my 1981 Ford Mustang as I drove as far as I could before spending the night somewhere between Cedar Rapids and Atlanta, Georgia.

My disposition was joyful until the sun disappeared below the horizon and daylight faded. I kept driving south until my eyes demanded a place to stop for the night. That place was Vincennes, Indiana, along

US Route 41. It was now dark. It was also windy and cold. I began to wonder if I had made the right decision. I wanted to hurry back to Cedar Rapids. That all-too-familiar sensation of intense loneliness bubbled up in my soul, but I knew that entertaining thoughts of turning back was not an option.

I was crossing my first career border and admittedly it was a frightening one.

Border Crossing #4: October 1, 1985

Being a part of The Weather Channel's start-up crew was a dream come true. National cable television was an exciting place to be in the 1980s. Bucking nearly every forecast that predicted TWC's demise in a year or two, TWC quickly became a cable television favorite across the USA.

More than three years after TWC's start-up, things changed at the network. I became restless and started to wonder if I had made the right decision when I earlier declined several offers to return to local market television, one at KUSA-9 in Denver and another at WISH-8 in Indianapolis.

At the right time, an opportunity opened in Minneapolis. It was time to pull up stakes and explore new territory.

Just before driving to Minnesota, I took nearly a week to drive to New Bedford to see my parents and siblings. This was immediately after Hurricane Donna pummeled southern New England. For the near weeklong visit at my boyhood home, there was no power. The house was so quiet and dark that it felt like we were living in pioneer days. I was hoping to stay long enough to witness restored power, but I had an appointment with another career border crossing.

It took two days to drive from New Bedford to Minneapolis. The second leg from Cleveland to Minneapolis was the longest. Determined to finish my journey in two days, I crossed over Lake Saint Croix and the Wisconsin-Minnesota border at exactly midnight. I caught something strange in my headlights. Dust? Ash? Pollen? Leaves? None of the above. It was soon evident that the moment I crossed into Minnesota, I was greeted by a snow shower. Even though I was driving alone, I began laughing out loud. How appropriate.

The biggest surprise about crossing this career border was the lack of second guessing or sentimental yearning for returning to the familiar. As I wrote in my book, The Extra Mile, I was tired of the summer heat and had my fill of grits. I never looked back. I was now a Minnesotan.

Border Crossing #5: July 1988

Even though Sally and I would have enjoyed remaining in Minnesota, there was one more career boundary to cross. While we had fun with a "husband and wife" on-air weather role at the NBC affiliate, KARE-11 on weekday mornings, a call to the weather office one morning changed everything.

Sally's mother called from Cleveland. She read in the Cleveland Plain Dealer that WJW-TV was still looking for a meteorologist for their start-up weekday morning newscast. Sally was under contract, but I was not.

"Do you want to go home," I asked?

That set the wheels in motion. Because long time weather icon at WJW-TV Dick Goddard knew me from The Weather Channel, he agreed to personally deliver my resume and video tape with his endorsement. I shipped them with express next-day priority.

Within a week or two, news director Virgil Dominic flew me in for an interview. It was a divinely timed meeting. By the time I was on my flight back to Minneapolis, I had a contract in my hand, ready to pray over and sign. I wondered what KARE-11 news director Tom Kirby would do when I told him about the offer.

Tom could not have been any more kind in his response. The bottom line is that he could not match their generous offer. He knew that WJW-TV had a reputation of hiring talent and keeping them long term. He encouraged me to take the job and contribute well, predicting that I would stay there for the remainder of my career in television weather. Furthermore, he told us that as soon as our house in Wayzata, Minnesota sold, he would release Sally from her contract obligations so that we could be together.

My first day at WJW-TV was January 16, 1988.
Cleveland's first morning newscast began on
Monday, February 8, 1988. Real estate is slow
moving in a Minnesota winter, but as soon as the
winter broke, the house sold and Sally's last day
was set as a Friday in July. Even though I was full-
time at WJW-TV, Virgil gave me the okay to join
Sally at KARE-11 for her last morning as the
"husband and wife" weather team. Pete and Mindy
Schenck, our closest friends, joined us at KARE-11
with their two young daughters who actually joined
me in the "News 11 Backyard," an outdoor weather
set that is actually attached to the studio via a
greenhouse set up.

After the KARE-11 morning show was over, the
hugs with Pete and Mindy were long and sad as we
prepared for the 18-hour drive to Cleveland. This
border crossing was different from all the rest in
several ways. Never before did we head for a new
border having to leave the kind of friends that the
Bible refers to as "someone who sticks closer than a
brother" (Proverbs 18:24). Even though we stayed
in close contact through these last three and a half
decades, it still left a chunk missing out of our souls
that could only be filled by back-and-forth visits.

The other aspect of "yearning for the familiar" also
returned. There was union unrest in Cleveland
with the real threat of a strike not long after we
settled in our new home. Up to this point in my
young career, I never had to deal with this kind of
discord. I began wondering if we had made the
right decision by leaving Minnesota. Career
"growing pains" were a big part of crossing into this

new land, not to mention feeling as though I was a very small goldfish suddenly having to swim in a very large, unfamiliar ocean.

Thankfully, a handful of my WJW-TV co-workers must have sensed my imbalance and rallied around me and encouraged me in ways that kept me afloat in those early years. I go into greater detail in my first book, The Extra Mile. I'm forever grateful for their love and care.

Border Crossing #6: May 22, 2024

What will this one look and feel like? I can only guess. Sally and I will be doing everything we can to make this next border crossing seamless and joyful. We want to avoid going through my final day like it's is a funeral. All too often, I've seen it happen and have expressed my desire that I want any underlying activities to be filtered through a lens of light and upbeat celebration so that I can focus on what God has called me to beginning on May 23rd. Stay tuned!

My guess is that will become this book's epilogue.

Thursday, April 4, 2024
9:16 AM, Cloudy, Damp, 34°F
Mile Marker 48

Jordan Scheufler (who graduates in May with an atmospheric science degree from OSU) received an offer from a television station in Twin Falls, Idaho!

I encouraged him to grab the first offer. Getting into the television news business is challenging. It is easier once your foot is "in the door." With my IPTV subscription, it will be fun watching him anytime I want.

Prophetic words out of my own mouth way back in 1994, thirty years ago, is forty-eight days away from fulfillment. Producer Chris Gibilisco (someone we call, "Jibby") found a story we did on the 1994 total solar eclipse. I remember it well. I had my six-inch Schmidt-Cassegrain telescope projecting a large image of the sun on a whiteboard on the station's east side (where "TV-8 Acres," my local TV garden was). While I don't remember saying this, apparently I said that the next big eclipse for us will be in 2024, marking my retirement from local television. Wow! Did I really say that?

I'll be a part of a segment we call Trending tomorrow evening when this will be replayed for my reaction. Little did I know that the first paintbrush stroke of this May 22 painting, now nearing completion, was made on THAT day, May 10, 1994!

Wednesday, April 10, 2024
9:31 AM, Cloudy, Damp, 49°F
Mile Marker 42

The synoptic painting of my career is almost finished. At this stage, I'm only putting accents on a painting that is largely done. If I dropped my paintbrush today, it would look fine, but the remainder of the accent strokes will (hopefully) elevate it from okay to memorable.

When I was still in elementary school in the late 1960s, I had a favorite page on the New Bedford Standard-Times daily newspaper to which I always turned first. It was page two. That's where I found the daily weather section. I remember drinking in every detail of the U.S. weather map, always looking for the potential of a memorable system to make weather-watching a bodacious affair. The nuances of the daily almanac along with its sunrise, sunset, and twilight times always had me dreaming of the cozy season of early sunsets. I can count on one hand the number of times I might have missed turning to page two over the course of more than a decade of my youth.

Eventually, with money I had saved over several years, I purchased a NOAA weather radio "cube" from Radio Shack. I was probably twelve or thirteen years old. It lived on the top of my dresser in the bedroom I shared with my brother, Denié. By far, that cube radio had more listen time than any other radio or television in our house. I remember transcribing the current hourly observations which were updated at ten minutes after every hour. To improve the signal quality, I designed a copper loop that attached to the top of the extension antenna with a metal alligator clip. Without that loop and clip, reception was sometimes impossible!

The cube did not follow me to college or to any of my television jobs, so I'm not certain of its fate. Now, some half-century later, I wish I still had it in my possession as a reminder of the endless hours of joy I received from weather analysis, but the memory of that simple weather cube will always make me smile.

Monday, April 15, 2024
8:22 AM, Partly Cloudy, 48°F
Mile Marker 37

When I step back to look at my word canvas as my career painting is almost finished, recent events are helping me to make more sense of this painting's significance.

While the career path, and everything that has come with it, has indeed been a gift of God, my very satisfying career in and of itself should never be the central focus of the completed painting. The career was only the glue that has bound together something far more significant. Each colorful stroke of the paintbrush is there because of a person and the unique and dynamic bond that God had purposed to weave it all together. The painting is coming into view. Every person who is living on the earth today, whether they realize it or not, is working on their painting. When mine is 100% done, I want mine to be in God's gallery giving glory and pointing to the One who is the author of every life, not because I had anything to do with it but because I was a willing canvas.

Wednesday, April 17, 2024
9:47 AM, Overcast, Damp, 65°F
Mile Marker 35

Today is my final official vacation day of my television career. Once I return tomorrow, my schedule returns to normal until I wake up on May 23rd. It will be time for a final clean up and clean-out. My final seasonal weather outlook (this one for summer 2024) will air at the end of the 6 PM newscast on Friday, April 26th. I told Sally that it would be fun to just make something up without the voluminous work of looking at all the quirky long-term parameters, but that would not be congruent with my career effort to do my best with the available tools.

There's a new live streaming web camera installed on the roof of Lyndon Institute at the bottom of College Road thanks to WCAX-3 in Burlington, Vermont! Seeing Lyndon Center Baptist Church brought back memories of my walking down from the college to attend one of their services. I can't remember when it was I did so, but it was likely in my freshman year. As best as I can remember, I was warmly welcomed. I think upperclassman, Joe Marcello, attended there and always encouraged me in my faith journey, especially after he saw me there. Despite my only going there once or twice in my four years in Vermont, his encouragement remained steadfast. The memory of that was indelible well past my college years. The last I recall, Joe had become a Pastor in Indiana but had hoped to break back into television weather. That was probably ten or twenty years ago.

Wednesday, April 25, 2024
10:22 AM, NACITS, 45°F (Morning Low 28°)
Mile Marker 27

I thought the "surreal" sensation of not having FOX 8 as my go-to weekday routine was behind me until this week. When that "Mile Marker" went below thirty, that surreal sensation returned.

My final seasonal outlook is on deck for tomorrow night. What kind of summer will we experience? Summers are not quite as "epic" as winters when it comes to long-range outlooks. That seems to be the case everywhere in the U.S.A. I wonder why that is? I think that's a case study for Scott Sabol!

There are two "major" ratings periods in local television news. One is in November, ending the day before Thanksgiving. The other is the "May book," and that one begins today, ending May 22 this year. Our advertising rate card is set according to the audience routines that emerge from these two important seasons. To exit my career on top of the ratings is sweet icing on a well-frosted cake (and yes, I like cake.... or almost anything sweet!).

Friday, April 26, 2024
10:02 AM, NACITS, Birds Are Singing, 54°F
Mile Marker 26

My WeatherJazz® audience has been privy to my upcoming chapter change for a while, but not the television audience in general. That all changes tonight on a segment FOX 8 calls <u>Trending</u>. With the help of Natalie Herbick, my plans to hang up my television isobars on May 22 will be revealed to the audience at large. This will open up the season of highlights and outtakes collected over the last 36-plus years!

All of the graphics for tonight's summer outlook are ready. It's a three-times-a-year exercise that has kept meteorologists at FOX 8 sharp. Not only do we all come to a general consensus about the upcoming season's "flavor," but since I am the one who fronts the effort on the heavily promoted segment, I am careful to craft maps and stats that are viewer-friendly and (most of all) interesting. While we individually have unique styles within our department, I realize that this triannual television event will likely "look and feel" different after my departure. I'm hopeful that I have influenced my colleagues with the methods and filters I've come to employ (in some cases learned the hard way) to keep this tradition fun and fascinating, both for the audience and the weather staff.

Audiences all across America love these super-long range outlooks even if their accuracy is only better than a professional dart-throw. Our attempts are improving every year as we understand the dynamics of global patterns. Even as a young boy growing up in New England in the 1960s and 1970s, my brother Denié and I rushed to the local New Bedford bookstore, Saltmarsh's on Purchase Street, to buy the newly released edition of the Old Farmer's Almanac to see what they were forecasting for our upcoming winter. Would there be snow for Christmas? How many nor'easters would we see? Denié and I would pour over every detail for weeks if not months.

I was nowhere near the only one to do the same. I suspect that because every person is affected by the atmosphere whether one was a truck driver, nurse, financial planner, or roadside construction worker, this glimpse into the future piqued everyone's interest. That's why Saltmarsh's (and all other bookstores) had plenty of copies on hand to sell. That general mindset hasn't changed in the last century or more. Call it atmospheric prophecy if you like, prophetic impressions get everyone's attention (although compared to the perfect Biblical prophecy, our atmospheric ones are only educated prognostications).

So what will the next FOX 8 Winter Outlook look like at the end of October this year? I haven't a clue! But you can rest assured that I will be waiting to see what's the FOX 8 weather team will craft. I'll be waiting (impatiently) just like I did as a young boy waiting to run to Saltmarsh's for our own copy of The Old Farmer's Almanac.

Saturday, May 4, 2024
10:24 AM, Overcast, 66°F
Mile Marker 18

I'm feeling delightfully satisfied that my career canvas is nearing the point at which I can put the paintbrush down and step back to make sure there are no empty holes. While there will always be times when, well after this book goes to print, I remember something that I wish I would have included, I have no hesitation to hand the reader what is a completed painting.

The mixed jumble of emotions has surprised me a little. They ebb and flow much more quickly now that May 22 is only weeks away. I suppose I should not be surprised. The mixed amalgam of emotions is strangely similar to other seasons such as high school graduation, college graduation, and the handful of career moves in 1982, 1985, and 1988. I anticipate a different landscape and a different pace along with new exploration challenges. I'm now bracing for Mile marker "zero," but I'm grateful that I get to bring my family and friends into the new state. Yes, I'll leave some things behind in my rear view mirror, but not my family and friends.

Tuesday, May 7, 2024
9:48 AM, Sun Disappearing, Clouds Arrive, 62°F
Mile Marker 15

Just before leaving the station yesterday, I told Lou Maglio and P. J. Ziegler a story about accents that had them amazed. It's a part of my early journey in the broadcast world that may be tucked away in a little, unnoticed corner of this canvas, but the implications on the big picture should not be dismissed.

The story takes place in my senior year at Lyndon State College when I was one of the five meteorology students involved in the production of three television newscasts daily. It was distributed in all of northeast Vermont on cable on Channel 2.

My wife Sally (who was then my steady girlfriend) raised a concern. As someone who was born and raised in Ohio, getting past my Bostonian accent was difficult. She made sense when she said, "If you want to get a television job anywhere in the nation, you really need to lose your Boston accent."

Sally helped me to lose that accent, but it wasn't until a trip home to New Bedford for our Easter break in 1981 that I realized how effective her coaching was. Instead of driving all the way back to Ohio for Easter, Sally came with me to New Bedford for the extended weekend break to meet my family. During the visit, my brother Denié suggested that we take Sally to Lukulos Pizza, a local pizza place that specialized in thick-crust pizza. I could not remember where Lukulos was, so I asked for a reminder of where they were located. My father chimed in, "It's on Knot Street."

Knot Street? Up to that point, I had lived in New Bedford all of my life and I could not recall any street called Knot.

After several back-and-forths, I asked my father for driving directions (long before the days of GPS guidance). After visualizing the route he was marking, I stopped him.

"Ohhhhh! Wait as minute! You mean that Lukulos is on NORTH Street!"

"Yeah, that's what I said," my father replied, "Knot Street!"

I suddenly realized that Sally's verbal coaching was far more effective than I realized. Not only was my accent largely gone, but I was not able to understand my own father!

This opened up the rest of the nation for me. I was now employable outside of New England. Imagine how difficult it would have been to get the attention of a television news director (Bob Jackson) in Iowa in March of 1981 when I was a month away from graduating from college?

Sally not only became my beautiful bride and life partner, but her gentle but effective communications coaching set me on a path to a successful career in both national television (The Weather Channel) and eventually a thirty-six and a half year tenure in Cleveland, Ohio.

Does anyone need directions to Knot Street?

Monday, May 13, 2024
8:01 AM, Partly Cloudy, 58°F
Mile Marker 9

This is becoming a bit surreal once more. This week is my final full week at WJW since mid-January of

1988. Yet in one respect, I am fully ready. Very few of my personal artifacts remain at the station. A photo of Sally and Noah on my desk is the most important item that will remain on my desk until it gets moved to a very small carry-out box just before I walk out the back door for the last time as an employee with three dear friends from northern Virginia. They wanted to surround me with love and support so that I would not swap out that mammoth-sized canvas alone. The more I think about that, the more "þakklæti" (I'll explain this Icelandic word in greater detail in just a moment) wells up in the center of my soul.

It started as a gift for my brother Denié more than a decade ago. I started collecting (and burning to CD) an episode from Casey Kasem's <u>American Top 40</u> from every winter, spring, summer, and fall from 1970-1979. Then I kept going after that initial collection was complete. I'm now approaching a complete collection while starting to work on 1980-1988.

I am placing all of those shows on a 1 terabyte SSD drive for the Tesla. When there isn't anything worth listening to on the radio or TuneIn, I can pick a week and year and listen to programs that I listened to the week they aired (mainly on 630-WPRO-AM, Providence, RI).

Why is it that men, in particular, like listening to what is now considered "oldies?" I still remember vowing to always stay "current" when it comes to music, yet I found it hard to embrace the music as I moved into the 90s and 00s. Every decade seemed to have its "sound," and I did not care a great deal at what I was hearing.

I believe I have just scratched the surface of realizing why it is I like listening to Americans Top 40 (particularly 1973-1981). It suddenly dawned on me that, as I was listening to each week's 3-hour program, I would find myself thinking about what I was doing as a high school and college student at the time. That eventually devolved into trying to envision what life would have looked like had I followed a different path.

I wrote about this phenomenon before from a different perspective. It goes back to the character Marty McFly in the now classic film, Back To The Future. The more you fiddle with trying to "go back" and "fix" regrettable choices, the more you realize that so many of the blessings you enjoy now would not exist.... the friends and family you have, the place you live, the place you work, and so much more. Would I be willing to give it all up?

About a week ago after everyone went to bed, I was securing the house for the night. As I turned off lights, switched on security systems, and checked doors and windows, I stopped for a moment and looked around. An indescribable wash of peace and satisfaction ("þakklæti" in Icelandic) overwhelmed me. I believe it was from the Lord, a supernatural kind of peace. In that brief moment of heavenly bliss, the definitive answer to the question, "Would I be willing to give it all up?," was a resounding NO WAY. The unhealthy tension between wanting to "fix" old regrets and living fully in the "here and now," disappears. God has a wonderful way of using anything you give to Him to His glory.

While watching Elijah Streams on Rumble a few weeks ago, guest prophet Kim Robinson brought to light the physical artifacts of not forgiving yourself for anything that God and others have already forgiven. I can attest to the fact that we humans are often the hardest on ourselves. Could it be that I had never fully forgiven myself for many of these low points in my journey? Both giving and receiving forgiveness is an act of faith. When forgiving yourself, you have to do BOTH! By faith, I joined Kim's prayer of self-forgiveness, declaring it out loud. Sometimes it's imperative to allow your own ears to hear your own words declaring something. Since then, whenever the enemy started whispering doubt, I immediately fought back, out loud, with faith-driven words of self-forgiveness. Why in the world would I want to cleave to an accusation that God Himself (and others) have forgiven? Am I equal to or greater than God? No. Not even close.

I still enjoy listening to Casey's Kasem's vintage programs while driving around, but lately I'm simply enjoying the music and trivia without getting caught up in the unsatisfying endless loop of playing the "what if" game that I wrote about earlier.

I wonder if it's one of the reasons why (men in particular) like listening to music from the era during which they grew up as a teenager, that is, the desire to make course corrections in life's journey? The antidote is best found in Paul's letter to the Philippians (3:13-14).

"I do not consider, brethren, that I have captured and made it my own [yet]; but one thing I do [it is my one aspiration]: <u>forgetting what lies behind</u> and straining forward to what lies ahead, I press on toward the goal to win the [supreme and heavenly] prize to which God in Christ Jesus is calling us upward." (Amplified Bible, Classic Edition, <u>emphasis mine</u>).

Wednesday, May 15, 2024
7:20 AM, Mostly Cloudy, 58°F
Mile Marker 7

I am truly humbled by the great kindness of many to wish me a happy and blessed retirement. I received a proclamation passed by the Ohio House from Representative Sarah Fowler Arthur (Ohio District 99) recognizing my thirty-six years of service to northeast Ohio. Wow! A personal notecard explained that she, as a very young person growing up, used to regularly watch my morning forecast segments at her grandparent's house. Before being elected to Ohio State Representative, Sarah was the first homeschool graduate in the nation to be elected to the State Board of Education!

I received a handful of well-wishes yesterday, one of them from special friend, Terrell Crawford and his mother, Karen. Terrell wrote to me shortly after

appearing in one of my first Canton, Ohio, Football
Hall Of Fame parades early in my career. He was
not quite five years old. He sent me a photo of
himself holding a sign that he held on the parade
route saying, "André, our favorite!" I still have that
photo today. Terrell is now forty and they will
continue to watch right up to my last day, just seven
days from right now. Terrell may have been
encouraged by many of our exchanges over the
decades, but it's people like Terrell that have
inspired ME time and time again.

"Iron sharpeneth iron..." (Proverbs 27:17).

And there's Sharon from Sheffield Village, Ohio,
who has enjoyed reading my entire Christmas In
Pilaf series and hopes that I will continue to write
more books in my new chapter. Rest assured, I'll be
sending Sharon a copy of this book when it's done
as my way of expressing my "þakklæti" and thanks.

One week from this very moment, I will wake up
praying for some dear lifelong friends, Kevin, Neil,
and Dawn, who will be driving to Ohio from Virginia
to walk me through my final hours at WJW-TV at
their insistence. Kevin (originally from Duxbury,
MA) was one of my closest friends as a college
freshman at Lyndon State College in 1977-78. We
teamed up as a radio duo on the college's AM
station, WVM, as "Handy Andy & Kaptain K" (okay,
okay, stop snickering, LOL). We look forward to
hanging out together on my first full day of my new
chapter with a new, blank canvas at Mile Marker 1
of the new territory.

Almost all of my personal artifacts are now gone from the station. Clearing everything out over the last few months was truly the way to go. Everything that remains will easily fit in a small cardboard box as I leave the back door as an employee for the final time. I'm now fully ready to enjoy the scenery of these last seven (miles) days.

Sunday, May 19, 2024
9:01 AM, NACITS, 64°F (Morning Low 51°F)
Mile Marker 3

As my final day at WJW-TV approaches this week, I'm looking at some notes about a dream on which I never really elaborated. I guess I'm still trying to figure out what it all means, or even if there is any meaning to it. The more time that passes, the more fragmented the images are except for a few. Those that remain as vivid as when I first woke up include anchor Tracy McCool powdering her face in the studio, seeing my longtime high school friend, Diane briefly near the stairwell door near the newsroom (she was headed downstairs for something), and seeing my "Aunt" Rita (who passed away a number of years ago) in the newsroom to express her pleasure of watching me reach a career goal. She looked so young and vibrant, the person I remember from my toddler years. Brother Denié was also in the newsroom asking if Amy Carmen (the wife of the late pop music star Eric Carmen) would be coming to my retirement party in the third floor conference room. Denié wanted to talk to her about gardening. (I'm still trying to figure that one out.)

The next three work days will zip past quickly. It all starts Monday morning as I visit the morning newscast (where it all began in 1988) during the 8 o'clock hour. Frank Arko, the owner of Rise And Dine, will also arrive at the station with breakfast for the FOX 8 crew. My only request is that he arrive wearing his famous doughnut pants!

Will we be pausing the final-day festivities for severe weather? It is certainly possible. As Sally said on Friday, talk about "going out with a bang!" I'm hoping for nothing stronger than garden-variety thunderstorms. My atmospheric order has been placed. Let's see if the atmosphere is paying attention.

Wednesday, May 22, 2024
12:00 Noon, Cloudy, 70°F (Dew Point 66°F)
Mile Marker 0

"The" day has arrived. I was up at 5:30 AM and watched a peaceful sunrise. Taking advantage of the sunny start to the day, I resigned to the fact that I would need to crawl under the deck to feed the garden house under the deck (essentially out of sight). Thank goodness for old t-shirts and grubby joggers.

After a refreshing shower, I ran the Tesla through the car wash and vacuumed it out in preparation for picking up Kevin, Neil, and Dawn at the Drury Hotel. They will be with me for the 3 PM party and the last two hours of my television career. Talk about special.

I wanted a prop for my farewell at 6:54 PM. Sally used to have painting canvases, but weeded them out after her season of painting was done. The new Hobby Lobby (formerly Mayfield Heights Walmart) came to the rescue! I placed a blank canvas, a painter's brush, and a tube of bright green acrylic paint in the Tesla's "frunk" to bring to the station. (The wisdom of KARE-11's Tom Kirby still resurfaces: "Anchors have hands.") Mission accomplished.

The atmosphere has honored my request. The thunderstorm that just clipped by Geauga County came close enough for frequent thunder, but no rain. The rest of the day should remain quiet and stable! Thank you, Lord.

My career painting is now done. I've put my brushes and paints down and it's time to place it in the gallery. I like what I see. Bold colors, vibrant lines, vivid imagery. I can't take credit for any of it, though. I may have stroked my hand across the canvas thousands of times, but all of those joyful colors made its canvas impact because of all of the beautiful people who kept those colors strong, rich, and radiant. Every person was God's gracious gift to me. I'm forever grateful (and thanks to Jesus, I will have an eternity to express that "þakklæti" to my Lord and Creator).

Yesterday, dear friend, Icelandic pop-star Jón Jónsson's congratulation video aired just before my weather segment. It has been people like Jón, Gunnar, Bill Martin, and so many others that are making this transition deeply meaningful.

When I wake up tomorrow morning, I will do so with something very exciting. A new, blank canvas! Lord willing, the canvas won't be empty for long. I suspect the colors with which I have to work will be just as interesting and as vibrant.

Now, time suit up and prepare to get my tie cut on live television for the final time, LOL!

Saturday, May 25, 2024
8:57 AM, Partly Cloudy, 71°F (Dew Point 65°F)
New Canvas Day #3

I was finally able to begin going through all of the cards and gifts that I received yesterday. I'm still amazed with it all. It makes the colors on the completed painting even more dazzling than I initially thought!

I'm toying with the idea of actually beginning to paint something on the blank canvas I bought at the new Hobby Lobby in Mayfield Heights on Wednesday. Perhaps a little here, a little there. Let's see what emerges.

Kevin, Neil, and Dawn are back home in Winchester, Virginia. Having them here for my last day at WJW-

TV, then hanging out with us all day Thursday made for an indescribable multi-day celebration. Our dinner together on Thursday night was, in my perspective, much more a celebration of Neil's successful defeat of brain cancer. Praise the Lord for His amazing gifts to us!

Tuesday, May 28, 2024
8:28 AM, Very Light Rain, 56°F (Dew Point 56°F)
New Canvas Day #6

I woke up this morning just as the dawn light was pushing through the overcast and wandered into the kitchen. I thanked the Lord God for this new day and began crafting the day ahead. With the Memorial Day holiday behind us, the new canvas became just a little "more real."

I received a delightful email from (now former) co-worker, news anchor Gabe Spiegel over the weekend. On his end, like mine, my absence from FOX 8 hasn't really "hit" him just yet. That reality, like mine, will come in increments until it is fully grasped, perhaps in a few weeks. Until then, how can I satisfactorily conclude the book I've been working on since last January? I see an epilogue forming off in the distance. I like what I'm sensing. It's forever wrapped with an overwhelming atmosphere of "þakklæti."

Since my wrap-up segment just before 7 o'clock last Wednesday, we've seen two severe weather episodes. My initial urge was to return to the

station to help my colleagues. Alas, my key card
into the gate and back door would prevent me from
doing so (not to mention my status change from
employee to former employee). I made a deliberate
adjustment so that I could enjoy the atmospheric
grandstand. Strange? Perhaps a little, but it's
exactly one of the changes to which I was yearning.
As Sally and I watched the extraordinary lightning
display in an open field last Wednesday night, I was
starting to regain the wonder with which the
atmosphere lured me into a career of tracking
weather events some six decades ago.

Wednesday, May 29, 2024
3:12 PM, Partly Sunny, 62°F (Dew Point 58°F)
New Canvas Day #7

You've got mail!

That's what WJW-TV assistant news director Marc
Singer texted me yesterday asking me if I'd be
swinging by the station anytime soon. I had little
planned yesterday, so I hopped in the Tesla and
drove to Cleveland. I felt odd without my key card
on a lanyard around my neck, but in all probability,
it was deactivated. Even if it wasn't, taking
advantage of a key card that is still active isn't my
style.

Once there, I buzzed the security guard, parked
near the security entrance and signed in as a
visitor. Now THAT felt strange! (The last time that
I signed in as a visitor was for my job interview in

December of 1987.) The security guard then let me loose to wander up to the newsroom unescorted, saying "I think you can find your way to the newsroom from here."

I brought the stack of mail home and opened it at the dinner table last evening and was both touched and amazed at the kindness and generosity of those who wanted to wish me well. One of the handwritten letters came from a sweet lady who is 95 years old. When her husband was alive, she said that they tuned in to see my weather stories every day. That was just one of the many stories contained in those moving cards and letters.

Spending a little time with Dontaé and Mackenzie in the weather office from my old desk (now occupied by Scott Sabol) was great fun for me, but realizing that they had work to accomplish, I tried to respect that boundary and kept my visit short. I'm looking forward to our more leisure lunch at a local eatery sometime this summer, a place and time my former colleagues can let their hair down.

Wednesday, June 5, 2024
9:47 AM, Overcast, Humid, 71°F (Dew Point 68°F)
New Canvas Day #14

Everything has germinated in "MM Retreat" (the name of my garden). "MM" stands for Mile Marker (instead of "Retirement," a word I don't particularly like). I also repotted the two pepper plants (red and orange) and they seem happy in their new patio container.

My new radio rhythm on WKJA-FM is going well thus far and I'm finding new and expanded ways to update AndreBernier.com on a more frequent basis. The new rhythm is still a work in progress.

Later today: Cancel my D.O. Summers dress shirt weekly pick up and purchase a glass water bottle (Walmart?) for the car now that we have a new water filtration system for the cold water under the kitchen sink. I would also like to finish designing the thank you base so I can begin sending out letters to people who took the time to send me "retirement" well-wishes.

Friday, June 7, 2024
11:14 AM, Eclectic Clouds, 64°F (Dew Point 52°F)
New Canvas Day #16

Despite staying surprisingly busy, missing my career colleagues of the last thirty-six plus years is something with which I am often needing to process. The pressures of working in a ratings-driven world encourages strong bonds to form upon the commonality of striving to be the best at telling stories, whether they are news, weather, or sports elements. I'm glad I am still on a text thread with my weather colleagues, but it does little to mitigate feeling set aside. They have moved on. If I'm truly going to start working on that new canvas, I had best do the same.

I'm looking for the right time, place, and method to write this book's epilogue, a fitting conclusion to what has been a several year process. It may take another few weeks, plus or minus. Okay, realistically, it may take several years, but waiting that long to place a bow upon this package will be too late.

Epilogue

I'm putting my paints and brushes down. Yes, I may second guess that decision with the desire to pick up a brush to tweak a part of my thirty-six year career canvas, however it's a desire I will have to use various degrees of willpower to squelch.

For anyone who missed my final ten minutes on WJW-TV (May 22, 2024), or you simply want to see it again or share it with someone, (as of this writing) I have created a web link that takes anyone to the video:

http://andrebernier.com/thatsawrap

This redirects to the video on my Rumble account.

I find it humorously ironic that, as I write this, Jordan Scheufler (I wrote about Jordan and his academic journey in becoming a degreed meteorologist earlier) has been training at KMVT-11 in Twin Falls, Idaho His very first commercial television debut is moments away. Jordan represents the final generation of many I had the privilege to mentor in this honorable career. But Jordan and I share two important markers. Like me, Jordan was offered his job in Idaho before he graduated from Ohio State. There are very, very few of us who can lay claim to this. Dumb luck? No way. Divine orchestration? Bingo. That brings me to marker number two. Like me, Jordan is faith centric, a committed follower of the

Lord Jesus Christ. As time matures him, I'm convinced that he will recognize God's Hand on every aspect of his life, even the details of his career just like me. Isn't it just like the goodness of God to give me this amazing gift, that is, to be a part of someone's career debut as I step away from the television camera?

The changes I witnessed and experienced since the mid-1970s, especially those in the last ten or twenty years, has been head-spinning. I cannot even fathom what awaits "the Jordans" of the world just breaking into the media business. It would not surprise me to see exponential changes in the years ahead. No matter how fast technology ushers us into new forecasting realms of yet not even dreamed, it's my prayer that this new generation of media forecasters will remember what drew them into this career in the first place. Former WBZ-4 (Boston) reporter Jack Borden, who started the non-profit group For Spacious Skies, said it best when he concluded every mail to me with one of two salutations: "Look Up," and "More Sky."

You don't need to be a meteorologist to appreciate either salutation. In fact, Jack challenged everyone he met to take the time to look up at the sky.

"If more people took time to examine the grandeur of the sky," he once told me, "crime would begin to disappear and people would develop soft hearts."

There were too any times when my own eyes were glued to the technological tools developed to study the very thing that is playing out in a daily drama right in front of our eyes: the weather.

I'm excited to have started on that new canvas of which I spoke on my last day at WJW-TV. I envision more books, more podcast episodes, and perhaps focusing own a few new hobbies in the coming years, Lord-willing. But I have found myself looking at and pondering the vastness of the sky much more regularly since hanging up the television isobars. Call it a time of rediscovery. I'm getting reacquainted with what drew me into what turned into an action packed career.

Let me get back to that Icelandic word to which I gravitated after hearing a song from my Icelandic friend, Jón Jónsson, titled:

"þakklæti"

which means

inexpressible gratitude, thankfulness, extreme gratefulness, ineffable appreciation

I smile with this gratitude as I box up my big collection of isobars. I may pull them out every now and then, but I suspect that most of the time I'll choose to sit out on the deck, pull up a chair, "look up," and get lost in the wonder of what God created for us too enjoy.

185

"The heavens proclaim the glory of God.
The skies display his craftsmanship."

Psalm 19:1 (New Living Translation)